IN FOCUS

PALMISTRY

Your Personal Guide

ROBERTA VERNON

WELLFLEET
PRESS

Inspiring | Educating | Creating | Entertaining

Brimming with creative inspiration, how-to projects, and useful
information to enrich your everyday life, Quarto Knows is a favorite
destination for those pursuing their interests and passions. Visit our
site and dig deeper with our books into your area of interest:
Quarto Creates, Quarto Cooks, Quarto Homes, Quarto Lives,
Quarto Drives, Quarto Explores, Quarto Gifts, or Quarto Kids.

Copyright ©2018 Zambezi Publishing Ltd.
Text © 2018 Zambezi Publishing Ltd.
Unless otherwise noted on page 156, illustrations © 2018 Quarto Publishing Group USA Inc.

First published in 2018 by Wellfleet Press,
an imprint of The Quarto Group
142 West 36th Street, 4th Floor
New York, NY 10018 USA
T (212) 779-4972 F (212) 779-6058
www.QuartoKnows.com

Wellfleet Press titles are also available at discount for retail, wholesale, promotional, and bulk purchase.
For details, contact the Special Sales Manager by email at specialsales@quarto.com or by mail at
The Quarto Group, Attn: Special Sales Manager, 401 Second Avenue North, Suite 310,
Minneapolis, MN 55401, USA.

10 9 8 7 6 5 4

ISBN: 978-1-57715-172-2

Cover and Interior Design: Ashley Prine, Tandem Books

Printed in China

This book provides general information on various widely known and widely accepted images that tend
to evoke feelings of strength and confidence. However, it should not be relied upon as recommending or
promoting any specific diagnosis or method of treatment for a particular condition, and it is not intended
as a substitute for medical advice or for direct diagnosis and treatment of a medical condition by a
qualified physician. Readers who have questions about a particular condition, possible treatments for that
condition, or possible reactions from the condition or its treatment should consult a physician or other
qualified healthcare professional.

This book is dedicated to the memory of Malcolm Wright, who was a wonderful palmist, artist, and friend.

CONTENTS

CAN YOUR HANDS UNVEIL YOUR FUTURE?

Barbara was bitterly disappointed. Her marriage was in tatters; she had lost her home and was almost broke. She could do little to help her family in either financial or practical terms, and her health was letting her down. She had spent money that she really couldn't afford to pay on a consultation with a highly regarded palmist. She needed some hope and guidance for her future, and on the decisions she needed to make. What she got was a deep and accurate description of her character, and while she'd found the reading interesting, it wasn't much use to her at that time. So what went wrong? Was this palmist a charlatan? No. The problem was that he specialized in reading character and personality rather than information about the ups and downs of life.

Hand reading does give information about the future, but within certain limitations because the whole of one's life is shown in one's hands, so questions about a current situation can be hard to answer. Most palmists, however, quickly develop a bit of intuition and even a psychic nudge as they learn the art, and later in this book I will suggest ways of adding a little magic dust to a scientific palmistry reading.

There are the things on a hand we can see "scientifically," without using any ESP at all. These are the evergreen topics upon which a palmist can throw light. As you will see, they all have a predictive element within them, so even a palmist who is as psychic as a brick should be able to answer questions on the following topics:

- Love and relationships
- Sexuality
- Money
- Business
- Career
- Aptitudes and talents
- Successes and failures
- Parents and in-laws
- Children
- Other people of influence
- Home and property matters
- Health
- Travel
- Pets

1

LOOKING AT HANDS

If you are even vaguely interested in hand reading, you should get into the habit of looking at hands and the way people use them. This is easy to do because you can observe others without them knowing what you are up to. You can watch celebrities on TV and ordinary people in any place, and, in time, the knowledge that you gain will show you that certain hands belong to certain types of people.

The illustration below is a map of the hand, and you will see it often in this book, wherever it is needed. A key to the astrological symbols that are shown on the illustration is also provided. (Please note, masculine pronouns have been used throughout this book for simplicity.)

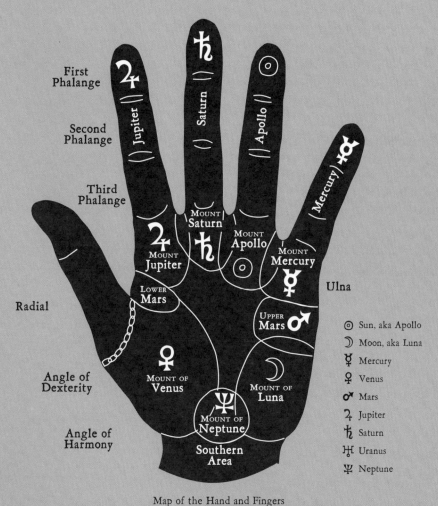

Map of the Hand and Fingers

History and Origins

Hand reading is so ancient that nobody knows how it got started, but palmistry as we now know it began to take off after the last ice age, when nomadic people settled into agricultural and village life in the Indus River region of northern India. Texts and illustrations that go back over 5,000 years refer to hand reading by the Sanskrit name of *Jyotish*.

Palmistry spread around the areas now known as the Persian Gulf, the Eastern Mediterranean, and the Middle East, and, in time, eastward into China and Japan. Whether something similar arose in other early societies around the world is anyone's guess, but we do know that Australian Aboriginal cave paintings show an early interest in hand shapes. It seems a fair bet that some members of every primitive society in existence would have taken notice of their own hands, and maybe some of those people endeavored to learn more about their meanings.

Moving forward a little, the Bible has various mentions of hand reading. Here is a very famous biblical quotation.

> *She is more precious than rubies; nothing you desire can compare with her. Long life is in her right hand; in her left hand are riches and honor. Her ways are pleasant ways, and all her paths are peace. She is a tree of life to those who take hold of her; those who hold her fast will be blessed. – Proverbs 3:12*

In 497 BCE Pythagoras wrote about hand reading. Starting in the thirteenth century, the expansion of the Turks forced Gypsy tribes to migrate outward in all directions, taking their fortune-telling skills with them, while the Crusades brought East and West into contact and carried new ideas from the Middle East into medieval Europe.

Napoléon Bonaparte was known to be highly superstitious and fascinated by all forms of divination, especially during his time in Egypt and the Middle East. Maybe it was his influence that created a renewed interest in the psychic sciences in France in the nineteenth century. Certainly the first modern books on "scientific" palmistry emerged in France in the first half of the nineteenth century, and toward the end of the century William John Warner wrote books on hand reading under the pen name of Cheiro, and his work is still in use today.

Since then, palmistry has grown in popularity and there is a lot of information available in books and on the internet. Even so, professional palmists are still few and far between compared to psychics, tarot readers, and mediums for the simple reason that it takes a great deal of time and effort to become a really skilled palmist.

Is It Palmistry, or Is It Hand Reading?

To practically everyone, the terms *palmistry* and *hand reading* mean the same thing. If one wants to be picky, one might say that palmistry refers to an examination of the palm while a hand reading refers to the hand as a whole, but whatever you choose to call it is really fine, because palmists read every part of the hand.

What Can You See?

You can see a great deal about a person's personality, talents, faults, failings, and the way he overcomes obstacles. There is also a great deal of information relating to the health of an individual at the time of a reading. One can spot events of the past, current events, and the way the future will work out, although it must be remembered that everyone has free will and that can change things. A simple example might be that if we change from an unhealthy lifestyle to a better one, the color of our hands and their general condition will show the improvement. If we walk away from a damaging relationship or a demeaning and depressing job, and make an effort to improve our lives, the lines on the hands change.

Enclosed Palmistry Wall Chart

Included in this book is a wall chart that contains the major areas and lines summarized from the following pages to be used as a quick and handy go-to guide for your practice.

❄ ❄ ❄

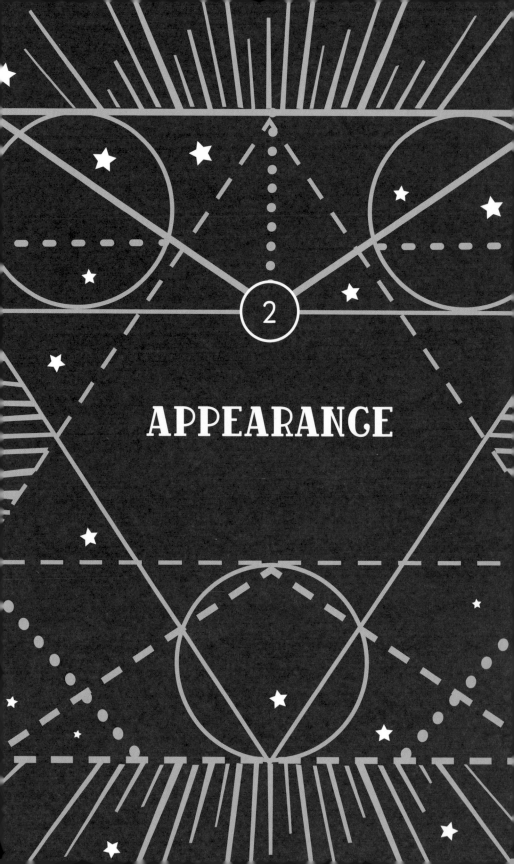

2

APPEARANCE

Large or Small Hands

Someone with large hands can cope with details and will be good at practical tasks, but he may become bogged down when it comes to looking at the wider picture. Small hands suggest an energetic person who gets new ideas off the ground quickly, but he may have difficulty in coping with details or seeing things through. If there is a discrepancy between the size of the hands and the size of the person, there will be a disconnect somewhere within the personality, so what you see may be different from what you get.

Square

A square hand denotes practicality. If any part of the hand is square, such as the palm or the fingertips, this indicates common sense and a talent for practical matters.

Long

Long, narrow hands denote an artistic temperament.

Rounded

Rounded hands denote sociability and flexibility but also a low boredom threshold. Some rounded hands are very basic, with only a few lines showing. These people are bright enough, but they may find life in general and family or other relationships particularly difficult.

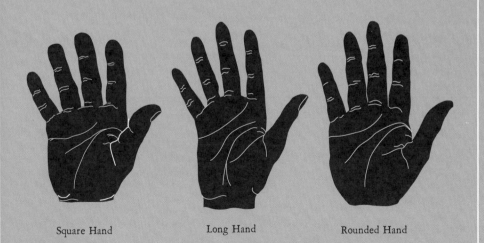

Square Hand   Long Hand   Rounded Hand

Knobby

Hands with knobby knuckles belong to those who love details and may have hobbies that take up their time. They think a lot, but they are introverted, fussy, and slow to take action.

Knobby

Angular

These hands belong to people who are independent and inclined to live life their own way. They are clever, inventive, and lucky as long as they don't wait for things to drop into their laps.

Many people have mixed hands, which makes it hard to be definitive about the hand shape. If the palm and the fingers don't match up, the personality is mixed, being partly practical and partly artistic, for example.

Angular

The Elements

Some palmists like to categorize hands by elements, and here is how that works.

Fire   Air   Earth   Water

Fire Hands

These have a rectangular palm or possibly a square palm with reddish or pink skin on the hands of Caucasians. The palm is longer than the fingers. There will be more lines on this kind of hand than the others, and they may be shallow and curved rather than straight.

Air Hands

These have rectangular palms and long fingers, possibly with knobby knuckles. They may have low set thumbs, and the skin is pale and often dry. The palm is the same length as the fingers. The lines will be a mix of curved and straight and there will be plenty of them, but they may not be as deeply indented as those on some other hand types.

Earth Hands

These are usually square shaped, with broad, square palms and fingers, coarse skin, and a reddish color. The palm is pretty much the same length as the fingers. The hand has few lines, but the ones it has are deep, well-defined, and may be straight rather than curved.

Water Hands

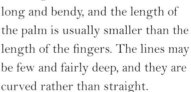

These long hands sometimes have a lozenge-shaped palm. The fingers are long and bendy, and the length of the palm is usually smaller than the length of the fingers. The lines may be few and fairly deep, and they are curved rather than straight.

OTHER POINTS

◆

- Heavy-looking hands denote physical strength, and if they are also fairly flexible with a heavy knuckle at the base of the thumb, the person is likely to be athletic. Hands with hard-packed flesh belong to someone slightly intolerant, who may be hard on himself and others.

- Someone with hard hands works hard, while someone with soft hands is weaker, tires easily, and may dislike hard work. Delicate hands denote less physical strength, but soft hands can also signify pregnancy, hormonal problems, old age, ill health, or a vegan diet.

- Prominent veins on the backs of the hands suggest sensitivity.

- People with smooth hands think and act quickly. Smooth skin signifies a more refined and sensitive nature than rough skin does.

Read Both Hands

Most people are right-handed, but many people are a bit of both. Even so, palmists refer to the hand we write with as the dominant, or major, hand and the other hand as the minor one. It is important to read both hands, as the minor hand can reveal more about the personal and emotional aspects of one's life.

- The minor hand shows the gifts that we were born with, while the major one shows how we adapt to changing circumstances.
- The minor hand shows the past and the major hand the future.
- The minor hand indicates emotional matters, while the major one denotes the practicalities of life.
- The minor hand gives more information on health than the major hand.
- The minor hand shows one's inner nature and often carries memories of past events, especially if they have been traumatic.

The Two Sides of the Hand

The radial side of the hand is the thumb side and the ulna side is the percussion side. Features on the radial side have more to do with worldly or abstract matters, while the ulna side is more concerned with feelings, imagination, and relationships. Palmists differ in the way they split the hand between radial and ulna, but either way is fine.

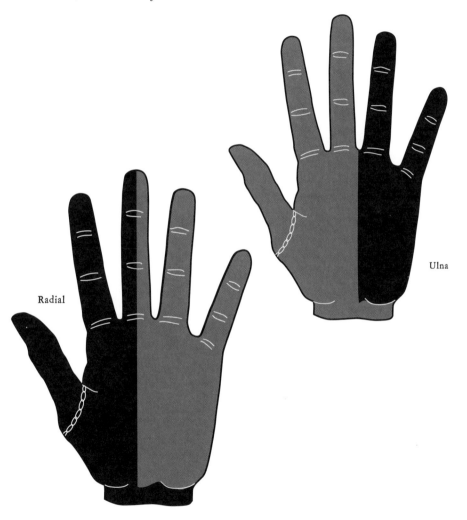

Radial and Ulna Sides of the Hand

Busy and Empty Hands

Busy hands have many lines and marks, while empty ones have few lines. The person with the busy hands has a nervous temperament, but he may have more endurance than one expects when it comes to coping with life. The person with this hand has a more active mind than the empty-handed person does.

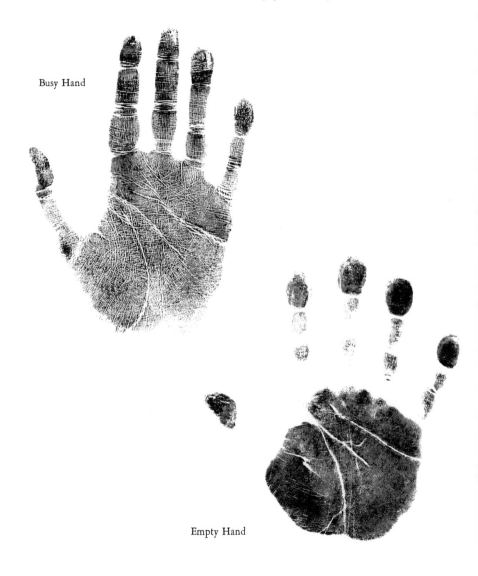

Busy Hand

Empty Hand

Hand Color

Taking racial differences into account, the color of a person's hands is usually an indicator of their state of health at the time of the reading. Sometimes a patch of color can indicate a specific problem related to health or something that is upsetting the person. Interestingly, a patch of color on the palm side usually suggests a problem that the subject causes himself, while a red patch on the back of the hand relates to a problem caused by an outside source. You will find more about color in the health section of this book.

What Is Normal?

Any line or feature may be longer, larger, wider, shorter, smaller, or narrower than normal, so it makes sense to have some idea of what "normal" looks like. The only way to do this is to look at as many hands as you can until you get used to hand reading.

3

FINDING YOUR WAY AROUND THE HAND

Way back in time, the palmists in ancient India named the various parts of the hand after the sun (aka Apollo), the moon (aka Luna), and the five planets that were visible with the naked eye, these being Mercury, Venus, Mars, Jupiter, and Saturn. The natures of the parts of the hand were linked to what was understood as the astrological natures of the planets. Over the years, the definitions of both palmistry and astrology have changed, but not as much as one might expect. In recent years, palmists have added Neptune to fill a gap that has long existed, and the idea works well.

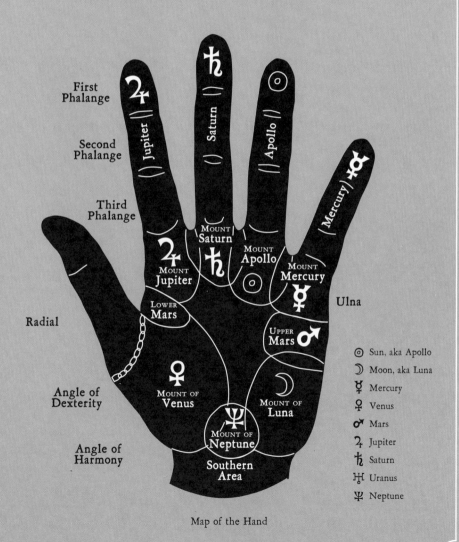

Map of the Hand

The Mounts

The areas that divide up the palm are traditionally called *mounts*, despite the fact that some of seem more like valleys.

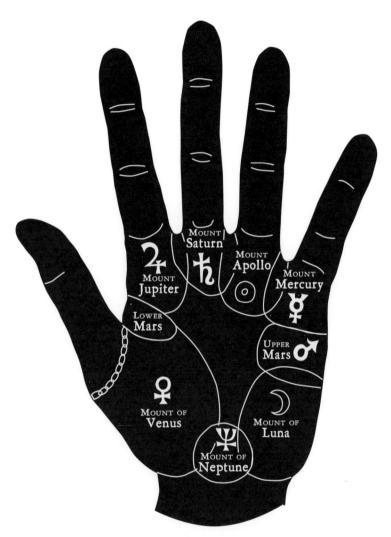

Mounts of the Hand

Mount of Jupiter

The Jupiter mount and the finger that
is above it relate to a person's self-
confidence and leadership abilities.
This mount can show teaching ability,
idealism, and an interest in legal
matters. It is linked to self-esteem
and, in a vague way, to wealth. A
high mount belongs to someone who
may be proud and arrogant but also
successful, while a flat one shows
a lack of self-confidence. A square
mark here shows that the person has
learned to protect himself from hurt.

Mount of Saturn

Saturn is mainly concerned with
practical matters such as security,
keeping a roof over one's head, and
necessities, as well as scientific or
technical matters and engineering. A
reasonably large area here suggests
the person will do well in business,
but he may also be interested in
politics and religion. The way
marks form here relate to how much
a person will enjoy security and
comfort in later life—or suffer from
a lack of it. If the area is fairly large,
the person will work hard and achieve
success through work, but if it is
shallow, with little space from the
bottom of the fingers to the heart line,
the person may be materialistic and
inconsiderate.

Mount of Apollo

The mount of Apollo is traditionally linked to art and music, but it also relates to creativity, pleasure, and to some extent home life.

If this is shallow and cramped, the subject may be a sourpuss who can't enjoy himself or give pleasure to others. A decent-sized mount shows the chances of happiness in later life, but it is also linked to home life, family life, the arts and music, and a desire to be happy and creative.

Mount of Mercury

This area is concerned with communications as well as health and healing, and marks here indicate a talent for conventional or spiritual healing. If Mercury is large and fairly full, the person is a good communicator, and he will have no difficulty working with new technology and engineering.

Mount of Venus

The mount of Venus is concerned with "plenty," meaning goods and possessions as well as affection. It shows a person's passions—or lack of them. Old palmistry books tell us that a person with a large and prominent mount of Venus is sexy—and he may be—but the truth is that he will definitely be *passionate* about something.

A wide and well-developed Venus endows a person with energy, sociability, and determination, and it is often an indicator of worldly success.

A flat or cramped Venus belongs to someone who is friendly but not really into family life, so he may prefer to live alone. This subject lives in his own head and enjoys solitary pleasures such as reading or listening to music.

Lines that are deeply scored and run across Venus into the hand itself denote interference in the subject's life by family members, in-laws, neighbors, and so on. A mark or wart on Venus is a sign that the person is worried about finances and security.

Mount of Luna

The mount of Luna is linked to the imagination, intuition and creativity. It also concerns travel and restlessness.

A prominent Luna indicates imagination and sometimes creativity. It also links with intuition and psychic ability, so a fair-sized Luna belongs on the hand of someone who can sense emotion that emanates from people, objects, or places. Conversely, if this area is flat and cramped, the subject won't have much imagination or intuition.

A sizeable Luna signifies a restless person who enjoys travel and adventure, so he may choose a career that takes him from place to place, and he may also travel for fun. A high mount with a curved line that runs vertically up and down through it often suggests psychic gifts or healing abilities. A high mount with a whorl or loop in the skin's ridge pattern can indicate too much imagination and a tendency to exaggerate and tell lies.

At the bottom of the Luna mount is a bone just above the place where the hand joins the wrist. If high and wide, the person is very restless, but if it nicks inward at the percussion edge, the subject may enjoy the occasional vacation but prefers to be close to home.

The Central and Lower Hand

The central area of the hand is devoted to Mars, but it is subdivided into upper Mars, lower Mars and the plain of Mars. The lower hand, between the mounts of Venus and Luna, are devoted to Neptune.

Upper Mars

Upper mars is on the outer, percussion, side of the hand and is concerned with courage and the ability to stand up for oneself verbally or even physically. If this area is high or if the side of the hand is thick, the person isn't easily taken by surprise, and he may be interested in the martial arts. People who wear uniforms for their jobs often have strong upper Mars mounts, and they enjoy being where the action is. Oddly enough, if this area bows outward on the percussion edge, the person has creative talent and he may work with his mind and hands in a creative manner. The only problem comes when this area is very heavy, as that person is unpredictable and may even be violent, especially if he is a drinker.

If this area is thin through the hand, the individual lacks courage and he will have a nervous nature. He hates when life rolls over him and makes him feel out of control, but he doesn't know what to do about it. This person may have suffered as a child, and he remains cautious or nervous throughout life as a result. If the thumb is set high and doesn't open out widely from the hand, the childhood was particularly difficult.

If the edge of the hand is straight rather than bowed, the subject could be a good record keeper, secretary, or analyst. He can interpret and improve upon the ideas of others, but he may not be creative in his own right.

Lower Mars

Lower Mars is often higher on the hand than upper Mars, which is confusing. It is found around and above the thumb in the area where it opens, and it is inside the life line.

Someone with a prominent, large, or high lower Mars mount is likely to have been a scout, military cadet, or something of this kind when he was young, and he may still be involved in this kind of activity as an adult. He may choose to do some kind of military service, and he will enjoy it. He is a good team member, especially when there is serious work to be done, and he may start or join political pressure groups.

A flat, indented, or cramped area here belongs to an individual who sees no need to join pressure groups or get into uniform, and he may be too individualist to be a good team member. Lots of crisscrosses in this area show a difficult childhood and a particularly bad time at school, all of which makes the person uninterested in team-building activities.

The Plain of Mars

The plain of Mars is the area in the center of the hand, and it is the part of the hand where many lines tell their story. If the area is fairly flat, the person is neither overly generous nor selfish and stingy. If hollow, something is odd about the person's attitude toward others, because he may give too much of his money or goods away in an effort to buy love and approval, or it may go the other way, making him tightfisted.

Neptune: The Area between Venus and Luna

This area represents the link between the conscious and unconscious mind, and it also connects the spiritual and the material world via practical and materialistic Venus and the imaginative and psychic world of Luna. Psychics, spiritual mediums, artists, psychologists, dream analysts, and creative people have a higher area here than those who aren't interested in these things. The area can talk about buried feelings that hark back to childhood and youth.

Angles

Angle of Dexterity

The joint at the base of the thumb is called the *angle of dexterity*, or the *angle of rhythm*. If it is reasonably well-developed, the individual is said to be dexterous and good at do-it-yourself jobs and engineering, but I have never found this to be the case. The angle is also said to convey a sense of rhythm, but I have not found that to be the case either. In my experience, a strong angle belongs to an actor, athlete, or anyone who uses his muscles for his livelihood. Timing makes sense here, but not necessarily rhythm. A flattish angle belongs to someone who is more mental than physical and more likely to be found writing, painting, or knitting than building bridges or lifting weights.

Angle of Harmony

The angle at the very base of the hand where it meets the wrist on the thumb side can be quite prominent and so low that it almost moves down into the wrist; this shows a love of music and melody. The individual may play an instrument, or he may simply enjoy listening to music or dancing to it. If there isn't much of an angle here, the person isn't into music.

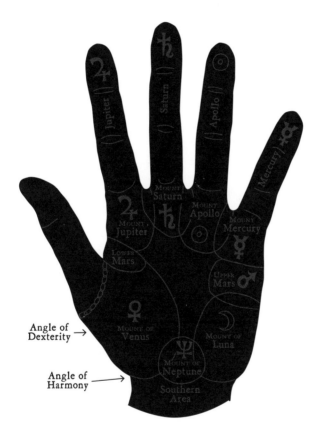

❋ ❋ ❋

4

THE FINGERS

Like the mounts, the fingers are known by their planetary names, as you can see from the illustration below.

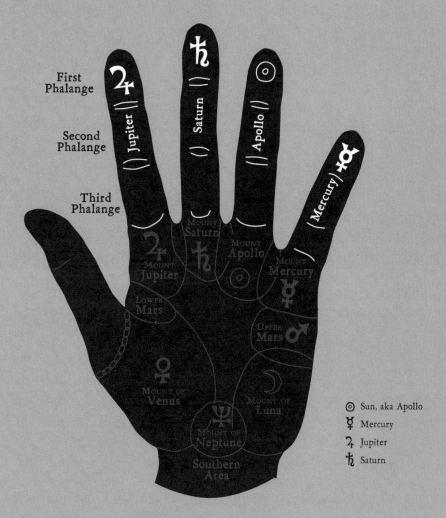

First Phalange

Second Phalange

Third Phalange

Jupiter

Saturn

Apollo

Mercury

MOUNT Saturn

MOUNT Jupiter

MOUNT Apollo

MOUNT Mercury

LOWER Mars

UPPER Mars

MOUNT OF Venus

MOUNT OF Luna

MOUNT OF Neptune

Southern Area

⊙ Sun, aka Apollo

☿ Mercury

♃ Jupiter

♄ Saturn

An Overview of Fingers

Over the years, I have noticed that fingers can change their shape and size, and not just as a result of arthritis. Someone who once had slim fingers but put on weight can end up with what looks like a bunch of sausages. The classic fatty hands and pointy finger ends of the obese person can become slender with rounded fingertips if the person loses weight. This may seem obvious, but it does have a secondary consideration. The hands are the first part of the body to touch the world around us, and the way we interact with the world is shown here. So someone who is more interested in food, drink, and their own needs doesn't develop the rounded finger ends of a sociable character until they change their thought processes.

Flexible fingers belong to a subject who is a team worker who can fit in with most situations. This person is outgoing and sociable. Bendy fingers are a common sight on nurses and others who care for others as part of their work and genuinely want to help people. Flexibility is also a sign of a traveler who loves to visit new places. Stiff fingers are seen on a more rigid type of person, who may be shy and somewhat uncommunicative. He may find it hard to appreciate someone else's point of view.

Short fingers denote physical energy and may show an "organizing" or bossy personality, while longer ones suggest a dreamy nature. Knotty knuckles belong to a deep thinker who is good with details and hates to be rushed, while smooth fingers signify less thought before taking action.

The Jupiter and Saturn fingers relate to public life while the Apollo and Mercury fingers are more interested in one's personal life. Consider a priest who uses only Jupiter and Saturn when giving a blessing; he is dealing with public matters and is concerned with his job. Winston Churchill's famous "V for Victory" hand sign is a similar manifestation.

Watch a person on television or in real life and see if any of his fingers sink down below the others as this will show his state of mind at the current time. For instance, if the Jupiter finger dips down, he lacks confidence, while if it is Saturn that is sinking, he is worried about money and security. If the Apollo finger is sinking, he may have domestic or property problems or is having trouble with some kind of creative endeavor, while if the Mercury finger dips, he may be suffering from a lack of communication, especially in his personal life. A hidden or tucked-in thumb describes a deep need to protect himself from mental or physical harm.

Inclination

The way that fingers sit on the palm can make them appear longer or shorter than they really are, so it is worth using a ruler or a piece of ribbon when assessing the true length of each finger.

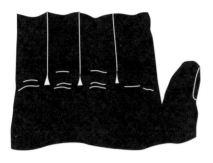

Straight Setting

When fingers are set in a straight line, the top of the palm is also straight, suggesting a measure of practicality. A creative person who lacks confidence has fingers arrayed an arc shape. Musical subjects sometimes have fingers set on a slope running downward from the index finger to the little finger.

The Way Fingers Lean

JUPITER

When the Jupiter finger pulls away from the Saturn finger, the person has a mind of his own, but if it pulls away too much, the person won't take advice nor will he understand the needs of others. If the Jupiter finger leans into the Saturn finger, the subject is unsure of himself and needs the support and encouragement of others. He can be too apt to listen to others, and he may believe their opinions have more validity than his own.

SATURN AND APOLLO

A V-shaped gap between Saturn and Apollo can suggest rebelliousness and an unusual temperament. If Saturn and Apollo cling together, the subject needs to feel appreciated and understood. He needs a fulfilling career and pleasant working conditions. He may choose to work in a field that gives him pleasure rather than working for a purpose, and he may not be driven by a desire for money. He tries to maintain a balance between family life, his work, and his belief system.

MERCURY

It is common for the Mercury finger to lean away from the other fingers, and this shows independence. While this person can work as part of a team, he prefers to have his own little job and his own area of expertise within the team. He may be slow to commit himself but steadfast once he does so. Bends and kinks in this finger denote obstinacy.

When people are extremely upset or in a state of shock, they peer at their fingertips almost as if seeing them for the first time. In some primitive way, the fingers are the first parts of ourselves that we seek to understand, and they form an important link between ourselves and the wider world.

The way people use their hands can change according to how they feel. For instance, a person who is in severe emotional pain will curl the fingers fairly tightly and will tuck the thumb in. The arms might be held straight down at the sides of the body.

Phalanges

If you want to be absolutely correct, the singular form of the word for this feature is *phalanx* and the plural is *phalanges*, but many palmists talk about a *phalange* as the singular—and so do I!

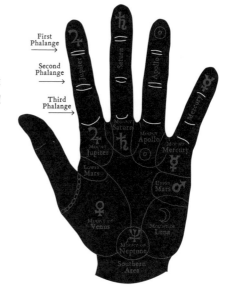

A phalange is one of the divisions of a finger. There are three phalanges on each Jupiter, Saturn, and Apollo finger, and two on each thumb. The Mercury fingers usually have three phalanges, but they can have two or even four small ones.

The upper phalange includes the pad part of the finger, and this relates to the way a person thinks, so it should be fairly long and reasonably high to show intelligence. A prominent top phalange with a pad that has a droplet shape indicates a talent for sewing, art, or craft work.

A long middle phalange shows that the person can turn ideas into something concrete.

The lowest phalange is concerned with security, so if this is full, the person needs money in the bank and a house that is mortgage free. If it is thin, the subject isn't driven by material concerns.

The Jupiter Finger

You can use common sense to judge whether a Jupiter finger looks strong and powerful or weak and weedy, but you might want to use a piece of ribbon to work out whether the Jupiter finger is longer, shorter, or the same length as the Apollo and Mercury fingers.

Strong Jupiter

The Jupiter finger rules leadership and the courage of one's convictions. A strong Jupiter finger usually relates to a strong personality and the ability to dominate others or at least steer one's way through a minefield of office politics. If the Jupiter finger is also long and well-developed, it belongs to someone who thinks well of himself, and, given a bit of luck, will see himself as a winner. He may have faith in a particular ideology or religion, thereby giving him the feeling that his ideas are the only ones worth having. Even if the person starts out as a junior team member, he will push himself to the top through determination, assertiveness and belief in himself.

If the finger is thin and delicate looking, the person isn't as assertive or aggressive, but he still manages to get his own way. He won't put himself out for others too much, and he may expect them to do his dirty work.

In many cases, the Jupiter finger looks short but it is actually low set. In these cases, the person can achieve a lot in life as long as he believes in what he is doing. He can succeed despite living through a difficult or unhappy childhood, because the finger is fundamentally strong. He isn't as fond of himself as the other Jupiter types, and he won't look like a winner to outsiders, but like the tortoise in the old fable, he will work very hard and eventually overtake all the hares to win in the end.

Weak Jupiter

When this finger is short, thin, or weedy looking, the person will look to others to take charge. He may prefer to be a servant or part of a group, and he won't want to stand out in a crowd. He worries about the way he appears to others, so he hides his light under a bushel.

Listen to Me!

••••◆◆◆◆◆••••

Leaders of religions and businesses, teachers, media moguls, and other self-styled front-runners are fond of pointing their Jupiter fingers and wagging them around. If you watch the kind of reality TV where couples or families fight and argue, you will see lots of Jupiters pointing and wagging as each individual fights for supremacy over the others. This subject doesn't care what other people think, because the only opinion that really counts is his own.

Saturn Finger

To modern palmists, this finger is concerned with survival and status, so concepts such as money, goods, position, and security are involved in this finger, along with religion, science, and some forms of political and ideological belief. Traditionally, this finger has always been linked with religion and morality.

Strong Saturn

Older forms of palmistry link a long, strong Saturn finger with a powerful belief in religion and a personality that is moralistic, prudish, miserly, and overly serious. This subject is said to have no sense of humor and no sympathy for others. He sets himself above others and considers himself very important. There is an ancient link with science and mathematics, and such things as accountancy and statistics are concerned here as well.

Modern palmistry doesn't argue too much with this definition, but in what are becoming increasingly hard times for ordinary people, a strong, fairly thick, and longish Saturn finger belongs to someone with common sense, who ensures that he and his family have their basic needs met. If there is a chance of gaining more status and a stronger position in life, this person will go for it, but it might still be by working for an organization such as a church, temple, or university.

This person has a powerful intellect and strong opinions. He will work for the things he believes in. He is careful with money, and he may look after the finances of others. He may be a good teacher or clever in some way, and he will have an imposing personality. Oddly enough, this subject may be happy to sit back on his laurels and avoid too much hard work as long as those he supervises do their job properly.

Weak Saturn

A short Saturn is a good indicator of talent for acting and media, and it can lead to considerable success. Alternatively, the person may find it hard to commit to long-term relationships, take responsibility for his own actions, or care deeply about others. He may be a gambler or a trickster.

Apollo Finger

Older forms of palmistry assign this finger to an appreciation of the arts and music, possibly due to its connection with the Roman god Apollo, who was a musician. Modern palmists also link the finger to the arts and music, but also to creativity and a pleasant personality.

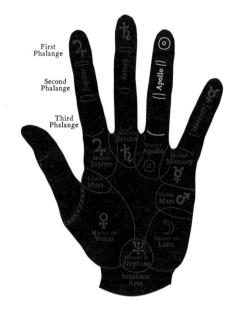

Strong Apollo

In recent years, scientific investigations using brain scans tell us that when the Apollo finger is long, the individual received an extra boost of testosterone while in his or her mother's womb. Thus when the Apollo finger is long, the person is said to have a talent for computing, mathematics, engineering, mechanics, and masculine pursuits. In short, the attributes that palmists have hitherto assigned to Saturn look like they should now be assigned to Apollo, thus forcing us to reassess a few millennia of hand reading in light of modern scientific advances.

Well yes . . . and no. This finger links with creativity and the ability to visualize, so it works well for actors, artists, engineers, journalists, architects, gardeners, designers, technicians, software engineers, and so on. Whether the implied masculinity also leads to aggression or a warlike attitude hasn't been validated by science or by palmistry, but while the Apollo finger could

Love, Affection... and Trickery?

A long Apollo finger signifies a person who is sensitive and emotional, and he may also be sexy, due to the fact that his needs and feelings are close to the surface. He will be artistic, musical, and creative. It is also said that someone with a long Apollo finger could become a successful pickpocket, which links it with thievery and trickery.

probably do with a bit of reassessment, don't let us throw the baby out with the bathwater. Whichever way you look at it, Apollo is linked with creativity.

Weak Apollo

It would be unusual for this finger to be really weak, but if it is significantly shorter, thinner, and weaker than the other fingers, the person has little interest in the finer things in life, and he may not want the responsibility of owning a home or looking after others. He may be dense and lacking in imagination, and he won't appreciate music or the arts.

Mercury Finger

This finger links with communication in the form of speaking and writing. It can indicate an interest in the healing arts, and it is said to have some connection to sexual behavior.

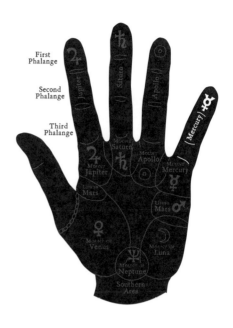

Strong Mercury

A long and well-shaped Mercury finger points to someone who will find and keep lovers due to his ability to talk, listen, and sympathize. This person probably has charm and a sense of humor. Sex is linked to this finger, and so he is likely an active and interesting lover. Little horizontal or diagonal lines at the very base of the Mercury finger denote an aptitude for statistics, figure work, and mathematics, but above all for teaching, writing, and other forms of communication. A Mercury finger that is separated from the other fingers belongs to someone

Mercurial Oddities

A series of horizontal or diagonal lines at the base of the Mercury finger denotes the ability to handle spreadsheets and statistics. Sometimes this finger has only two dividing lines across it rather than the usual three, and I have even seen four on occasion. All of these people have been good at working in a financial field.

If the Mercury finger hooks upward, rather like the old-fashioned way of holding a teacup, the person can be so determined to have his own way that he is pigheaded. When this finger bends outward, the subject is charming.

who isn't very sociable and likes the company of just his own family and a few close friends. He may be a nervous person who finds people threatening and difficult, so he may prefer pets to people.

Weak Mercury

A short or weak-looking Mercury finger makes it difficult for the subject to express himself, and it may cause problems with reading and writing or mathematics. A twisted, weak, or peculiar-looking finger might indicate some kind of sexual problem or signal a lack of interest in love making. When the Mercury finger is very short, twisted, or in some other way misshapen, the person's mind may be wired in an unusual way, and he may lack a sense of proportion. For instance, when the Mercury finger bends inward, the person may be argumentative, obstinate, difficult, or careful with money to the point of lunacy. He may also be untrustworthy.

TREE FROG HANDS

Have you ever seen a nature documentary featuring those little tree frogs that stick to things by means of little suckers on their digits? Well, there are hands that remind me of those little frogs. The hands are small and soft with a percussion that bows outward. The fingers are small and slim, apart from the first phalanges which are slightly rounded, giving the whole hand a "froggy" look. In every case that I have come across, the person who owns these hands is gentle, intelligent, and pleasant company, but untrustworthy where money is concerned.

Fingertips

Square Tip

Square

Square shapes denote practicality, so a subject with square-shaped fingertips and fingernails has a practical nature, but he may lack imagination. This subject may work with his hands or as a farmer or engineer, especially if the fingers are thick. If they are thin, he will have an aptitude for numbers.

If the tips and bases of the fingernails are also square, this will emphasize the tendency to see everything in black and white. If there is a discrepancy between the nail and fingertip, two different characteristics merge, so the person will be creative or sociable as well as practical.

Rounded Tip

Rounded

Rounded fingertips denote sociability and a need for variety in life. This subject gets along well with people, and he can be quite amusing company. He is generous and kind, but also a little lazy—or perhaps just laid-back. The best description for this person is *normal!*

Oddly enough, those who have rather short and fat fingers with rounded tips are often very musical, and they will play an instrument for fun or as a career.

Pointed Tip

Pointed

Pointed fingertips belong to someone who likes to do things his own way. He may eat or drink too much, or he may be into drugs. He may insist on living in a style that is very different from that of his family, and if he comes from a religious or moralistic family, he will go completely the other way. These fingers can denote sensitivity and artistic talent, but this person sometimes finds life hard to cope with, especially if the pads of the fingers are rather flat. This subject has strong beliefs, and he can be hard to influence, so he is probably idealistic and somewhat impractical.

Spatulate

When the fingertips are slightly splayed out they are called spatulate. This person is original, artistic, and possibly also musical. He has a strong inner spiritual urge, perhaps also a humanitarian one, but he will prefer an unusual life and likes to be among people who are creative, inventive, and interesting.

Spatulate Tip

Both the pointed finger and spatulate finger types can be extremely successful in a creative or artistic endeavors, but they can also be dreamy. Spatulate fingers can suggest self-centeredness or an argumentative personality.

Fingernails

The rules for fingernails are similar to those for fingertips.

- Square nails suggest an ability to cope with figure work and computing, and they can denote practicality.

- Rounded nails belong to friendly, sociable people.

- Narrow nails that show flesh on either side of the hand suggest sensitivity, vulnerability, and caution.

- Wide nails can denote a harsh or bullying nature.

- Fan-shaped ones denote ambition and a lack of concern for the feelings of others.

Thick or Thin

Thin fingers belong to those who are brainy and possibly artistic, but they lack physical stamina and may not finish what they start. Thicker, heavier fingers denote energy and stamina. These people are practical and prefer activity to vague ideas. They may also be very musical.

Fingerprints

The Loop

The loop is the most common type of fingerprint, and it belongs to someone who likes novelty and enjoys the company of others. Loops are called *ulna loops* when they enter the finger from the outer side of the hand and *radial loops* when they enter from the thumb side. Ulna loops are common, while radial loops are less common and they usually occur on the Jupiter finger or sometimes on the Saturn finger. A radial loop on Jupiter suggests leadership qualities, while a radial loop on Saturn indicates an ability to work with one's hands, perhaps as a carpenter, metalworker, jeweler, dressmaker, musician, or craftsman.

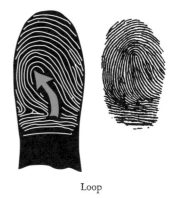

Loop

Arch or Straight Lines

An arch or rows of straight lines across a fingertip are common features, but they rarely show up on all the fingers at once. The arch belongs to a hardworking person who lacks confidence. When on the Jupiter finger or thumb, this demonstrates a difficult start in life and a family that didn't give the subject any opportunity to develop self-esteem.

Arch

The Tented Arch

The tented arch suggests the person goes "over the top" in some area of his life, and if it's on the Jupiter finger, this suggests fanaticism about a cause or some type of ideology. Tented arches can be seen on the hands of those who fall in love and then hang on when the relationship is clearly over. This is especially so when this arch is on Apollo or Mercury.

Tented Arch

The Whorl

A whorl on any finger indicates a measure of talent in the area of life related to the finger, while whorls on all eight fingers and both thumbs would belong to someone who is very successful or someone who was born with a silver spoon in his mouth and never needs to make an effort in life.

A whorl on the Jupiter finger denotes independence, determination, a go-getter attitude, and possibly selfishness. On Saturn, it can indicate talent in some practical field, while on Apollo it denotes artistic ability. On Mercury it suggests communication skills.

Whorl

The Peacock's Eye

This is a combination of a loop and a whorl, and it is a somewhat unusual fingerprint. It usually appears on the Apollo finger, suggesting artistic or musical talent, but it can also indicate a talent for homemaking, crafting, or gardening. If on Mercury, it denotes a talent for public speaking and writing. This person may also be an excellent counselor, nurse, or care assistant. A peacock's eye on the Saturn finger shows talent in a practical field such as technical drawing, carpentry, building, or civil engineering.

Peacock's Eye

Composite Patterns

This may refer to a double loop or double whorl, both of which are uncommon patterns that are rarely seen on more than one or two fingers at the same time. This person might find it hard to make decisions, because both logic and intuition operate at the same time, and this can confuse an issue. It is useful, however, for those who work in the psychic sciences because it shows an ability to deal with spiritual or psychic matters as well as practical ones.

Composite

OTHER FINGER FEATURES

- When all the fingers are widely spaced at the base, the subject may be a spender, and when allied to a short middle finger, the person might also be a gambler.

- Fingers that are tightly packed at the base and held closely so that no light can be seen between them demonstrate a closed mind.

- Fingers that fall away from other fingers suggest independence in the areas shown by the fingers in question.

- Those with fingertips that turn up at the ends often work for the benefit of the public. Nurses often have such fingers. These people also like travel and novelty.

- Fingers that are flexible at the base denote a person who loves to travel for pleasure, business, or both.

An Elemental Oddity

In the west, we align the fingers to planets, but hand readers don't bother to link star signs and elements to the planets. If we did so, this is how the system would look:

Finger and Planet	Sign	Element
Jupiter ♃	Sagittarius ♐	Fire △
Jupiter ♃	Pisces ♓	Water ▽
Saturn ♄	Capricorn ♑	Earth ▽
Saturn ♄	Aquarius ♒	Air △
Sun, aka Apollo ☉	Leo ♌	Fire △
Mercury ☿	Gemini ♊	Air △
Mercury ☿	Virgo ♍	Earth ▽

The Chinese do link the elements to the planets, although their ideas are somewhat different to those in the West. This is the system in use in some forms of Chinese palmistry:

Finger and Planet	Element
Jupiter ♃	Water ▽
Sun, aka Apollo ☉	Fire △
Saturn ♄	Earth ▽
Mercury ☿	Air △

5

THE THUMB

The thumb is concerned with strength of personality and willpower, although the lower phalange focuses on logic. A square tip to the thumb indicates practicality, a rounded one denotes sociability, a pointed one shows idealism, and a spatulate tip denotes independence.

A strong-looking thumb predicts determination, strength of purpose, and inner toughness. This subject is competitive. He may be a winning athlete, an entrepreneur, a successful salesman, or just have a powerful personality. A very thick, strong thumb shows a quick temper. A weak-looking thumb signifies a dearth of stamina and tenacity, along with a less-competitive nature. A very thin thumb suggests a nervy nature, and a short thumb shows a lack of courage. When the thumb is set low on the hand it will open out widely. This belongs to a strong and open personality of a sportsman, activist, actor, or politician. A high-set thumb won't open out as widely, indicating shyness and a private type of personality. Someone with a high-set thumb who tucks his thumb into his fingers is extremely nervous. If a child does this, it is an indication of insecurity.

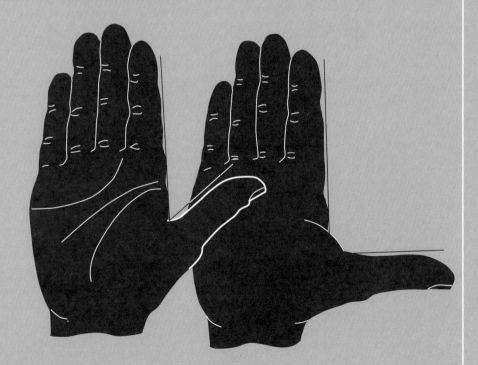

High and Low Settings

A person with a heavy knuckle joint at the base of the thumb needs a physical outlet such as sports, athletics, dancing, or working out. If the thumb is weaker but the base knuckle still prominent, he will be an observer of sports and activities rather than a participant. A thumb that is stiff at the base and can't be waggled around belongs to someone who digs their heels in and doesn't give way.

The Phalanges

The Upper Phalange

This phalange relates to willpower, so it is better for a person to have a fairly long and well-made phalange here. When the ball-joint phalange is powerful looking, the subject is strong-willed, energetic, and determined. Even if the thumb is not large, a healthy-looking ball joint indicates strength, willpower, and determination. When this phalange is rounded and medium-sized, the person is cooperative and pleasant. When flat, the subject lacks physical strength, and he may give way to please others. If the nail side of this phalange is indented or spoon-shaped, the person chisels away until he gets what he wants.

Sometimes the upper part of the thumb turns back. This is the sign of someone who puts on an act. This may be a professional performer, actor, or someone who

has to put on an act as part of his job. In his private life he is manipulative and may be a liar. This subject can be lazy or easily bored, but he is also impulsive and he likes to treat himself well.

The second phalange is concerned with logic. If it is long, the subject thinks deeply and he thinks before acting, but when it's short, he will act quickly and with little thought—he may act on instinct. A thin phalange of logic with a shape like an hourglass "waist" suggests a logical mind and deep thinker, but also someone who wants others to like him, or at least tolerate him.

The Clubbed Thumb

Some thumbs have a top phalange that looks like a club, and old-time palmistry books used to call this a "murderer's thumb." This isn't borne out by modern research, but this person does have a quick temper.

Temporary Lines

Quite often, you will see little vertical creases on some or all the phalanges, and these come and go depending upon the state of mind or health. Many vertical creases signify that the person is exhausted and overdoing things. Horizontal lines indicate that the person has more responsibilities than he can cope with and he may be worn out. Horizontal lines on the fingertips indicate some kind of hormonal change, activity, or imbalance in the body.

OTHER THUMB FEATURES

- A whorl thumbprint foretells willpower, determination, and independence, while a loop denotes a normal, sociable character who enjoys being part of a team.
- The arch belongs to a hard worker who fears poverty.
- The tented arch belongs to someone who gets worked up over nothing.
- The peacock's eye is a rare formation on the thumb, but when it does appear, it indicates talent.
- The double loop suggests a combination of intuition, logic, and psychic ability—and indecisiveness.
- Lines across the lower phalange suggest fatigue and perhaps an unstable home life or many changes of location. If life settles down again, these lines melt away.

THE LINES ON THE HAND

THE MAJOR LINES

When people realize that you are a palmist, they will hold their dominant hand with the palm upward, expecting you to look at the lines on their hand, because that's what most people think palmistry is. We already know that there is far more to hand reading than the lines, but nevertheless the lines are very important and they are also the only hand feature that can predict the future.

Hands change a great deal from childhood onward, as more data gets recorded and other data fades away over time. The condition of each line can tell the palmist a great deal about a subject's past, his life at the time of the reading, and what is likely to happen in the future. Generally speaking, strong, deep lines show vigor and health, while weak or fine lines show a nervous disposition or weak health.

The three main lines are the life line, the head line, and the heart line, but other lines are also important. Lines can be incomplete or they can be displaced from their correct positions, and this makes it hard to match some hands with the illustrations in this book. For instance, the fate line is useful for predicting events that concern the career and finances or the start or end of relationships. However, there so many variations in the line that it can be difficult to read. In some cases it isn't present at all!

EMPTY OR FULL HANDS

The best kind of hand is one that has some activity but not too much. An empty hand may only show the three main lines, and while this can belong to someone who has a very simple life, this kind of hand can also belong to someone who is deeply unhappy and can't find a way out of his misery. This hand is hard to read.

A full hand is said to belong to a neurotic personality, but it can simply show that the person has a lot to contend with and that he tries hard to do so. Someone with a full hand may also be a worrier. Hands that are covered in fragmented lines are hard to read.

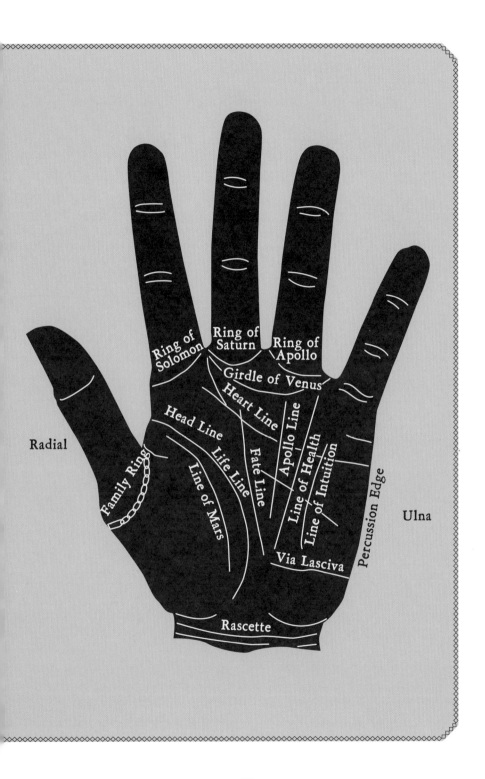

Radial

Ring of Solomon

Ring of Saturn

Ring of Apollo

Girdle of Venus

Heart Line

Head Line

Apollo Line

Life Line

Fate Line

Line of Health

Line of Intuition

Family Ring

Line of Mars

Via Lasciva

Percussion Edge

Ulna

Rascette

6

THE LIFE LINE

L et us start by looking at the life line, which is concerned with the subject's health, vigor, and the main trends of his life. The life line starts somewhere above the thumb, heads toward the wrist, and ends somewhere on the lower part of the hand. It can wander about or even break into pieces, and everything on it foretells something interesting that will happen in a person's life.

A Long, Strong Line

A long, strong life line is an indicator of health and vitality, but a short life line doesn't necessarily indicate a short life.

Curving in or Wandering Out

A long life line that bows out into the hand and forms a large mount of Venus (a) denotes passion and a desire to live life to the fullest. If the line is more straight than bowed and creates a small Venus mount (b), the person is a thinker and dreamer and he is less apt to pour energy into making money. He is also less apt to push others into doing his will. If the line bends around the base of the thumb, home life is important and the subject may choose to live close to his place of work.

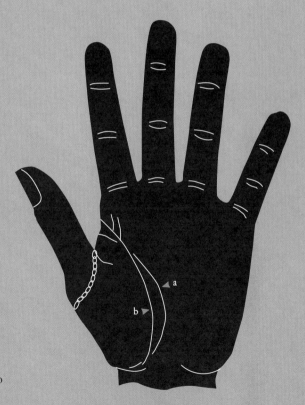

Types of Life Lines

When the line travels out into the hand, the career may take precedence over home life or the subject may travel a great deal for business or pleasure. Whether he chooses to concentrate on work or is forced to do so by circumstances is immaterial, the line simply shows the facts of the matter. Alternatively, the individual may move away from the place of his birth, but if there is a piece of line that curves around Venus, he'll probably retain an interest or a foothold in his old area.

The Start of the Life Line

The life line can start high up on the hand with a branch or two reaching up to the mount of Jupiter; this brings idealism and a cool, logical personality. If it starts lower down, it suggests a more practical and sociable attitude, but a more emotional personality.

Clear or Messy

A clear line here with no extra lines or "mess" around the starting area suggests a happy and comfortable childhood without any particular problems. If the start of the line is messy, the person's early life was difficult.

Islands occur when a line splits into two, thus forming an "island" in the gap. They are very common features on any of the lines.

Islands on the early part of the life line indicate early health problems or emotional traumas, while a fine line that falls down from the life line can denote the loss of someone who is important to the subject through death, divorce, or some other circumstance. A quick guide to determining the timing of youthful events is to drop an imaginary line down from the middle of the Saturn finger to the life line, because the part of the line that precedes this point relates to around the first twenty years of life.

A mass of small lines between the life line and the head line in the early stages of these lines talk of something wrong in the childhood—usually at school. The child might have been bullied by other children or was unpopular with his teachers. Whatever the problem, he was probably eager to leave school and go his own way as soon as possible. Sometimes the problem isn't at school but at home, and in this case, school was a refuge from a rotten situation. In really bad cases, neither school life nor home life was good.

Tied or Separate

The start of the life line can be joined to the head line, or it can be separate from it. Old-time palmistry books stated that a "tied" line meant the person stayed with his parents for a long time before becoming independent, while a separated one left home early. What does seem to be the case is that the "tied" person either chooses to stay close to his parents or has problems with his family that continue for many years. The separated-line person either chooses to be independent or is allowed to be their own person even while remaining close to the family.

Islands on the Line

An island on the life line points to a period of difficulty with one's health, a relationship predicament, a financial worry, a property problem, a matter of business, or practically anything else. A short, fattish island indicates a single event that had a real impact on the person, but a long one suggests an extended period of aggravation.

When the line splits into parallel lines along a fair part of its length, and when the lines are very close together—say only a millimeter apart—this suggests a long period in which the person is trying to cope with two situations at the same time, or he is just very busy. Someone coping with a demanding job, a busy farm, or running a time-consuming business while dealing with a hectic family life at the same time would have a life line like this. Another common cause is when a subject makes sacrifices for the sake of someone else, perhaps a handicapped person or a partner who is studying for a career and thus unable to support the family for a while.

If any kind of island is followed by a small line that rises up from the life line, the person will experience a period of difficulty, but he then makes an effort to improve matters.

The End of the Line

A life line can make a clean journey down the hand and curve around the mount of Venus and end there, or it can do a variety of other things. Regardless of the condition of the line, if it curves round Venus, the person stays close to his roots. Someone in a farming family or family business that everyone works in would have a line like this. Similarly, someone with a line like this is more interested in home life than a career outside the home.

When the line wanders away, the subject will move away from the area of his youth, and he may eventually lose all connection with it. He may go overseas or move to another part of his own country, but he will drift away from his roots. Another possibility is that the individual is more into his career than domestic and family life.

A Forked Line

A fork means a foot in both camps, so the person may live away from the area that he grew up in but come back from time to time or keep a connection with his family. Another reason for a fork is that the subject lives a full life with equal emphasis on home life and his career. If one prong

A Dangerous Sign

In some cases, an exceptionally short line on one hand indicates a near-death experience. I remember a case where a woman had nothing more than a stump of a line on her minor hand, and when I asked her about this, she said she'd been extremely ill as a small child and hadn't been expected to live. The fact that there was a normal life line on her dominant hand showed that she had recovered and would live a full life.

of the fork reaches out to Luna, and if the mount of Luna is well-developed, travel will feature in his life.

A long, narrow fork shows a struggle in life, because the energies of the life line are split, suggesting that the person is trying to cope with two demands at once. A typical scenario is that of a parent who brings up children alone. This kind of fork will be so narrow that it almost becomes a double life line.

A life line that ends in a tassel or shreds itself suggests a longish period of some bad health before the person dies, meaning the death is unlikely to be sudden.

Long and Short Lines

Most of us have ups and downs in life, and these will show up as breaks in the line, bars across it, and islands somewhere along the way.

Fortunately, the length of the life line bears no relation to the length of a person's life. Short life lines are often caused when the line breaks and moves over to start again farther down the hand, so that it is either displaced to the radial or ulna side. The reason for this is an event that derails a person's life for a while, and it could be caused by a disaster or something good, but whatever happens, it will be memorable and change the direction of the person's life. Typical examples might be the breakup of a marriage or partnership, a major job change, a difficult legal situation, a move of country, or an important house move. Winning the lottery can also change someone's life in a big way.

If a new piece of line forms on the radial (thumb) side of the hand, a new

Short or Disturbed Life Line

home will be in the offing, but if it forms outward toward the center of the palm (the ulna side) the career will take precedence.

Disturbances on the Life Line

Disturbances on the life line are common, so if you spot an island, a bar that cuts across it, or any other disturbance, check out both hands. Trauma often appears more strongly on the minor hand or appears to go on for a longer time. The problem could be one of health, a relationship matter, a financial problem, a legal problem, or a career one. It could even be the result of a war situation or a need to move from one country to another due to circumstances beyond the subject's control. Whatever it is, he will certainly remember it.

Lines that rise up from the life line after an island show self-motivation and an effort to overcome the difficulty or recover from it and improve one's life. Lines that fall away in a downward direction relate to things that have run their course. This might refer to people, things, or circumstances that drop out of the person's life.

Island on the Life Line

Pits

Tiny pits on the life line tell us that something is wrong with the spine or its surrounding muscles, ligaments, and tissues. If you look at the line as the spine, pits near the start of the line talk about pain in the cervical spine area, pits lower down can denote problems in the thoracic area, then the lumbar area and sacral area.

Parallel, or Shadow, Lines

Sometimes another line will run parallel, or shadow, the life line on the Venus side. This may be called a *line of Mars*, a *median line*, a *sister line*, or a *shadow line*. This offers protection from illness and accidents, so those who have this extra line are less inclined to fall sick or catch viruses.

These lines are said to show the presence of spiritual guides or ancestors who help the subject from "the other side." It can also indicate spiritual protection or a spiritual pathway that leads the person into interests such as hand reading, healing, clairvoyance, and so on.

The Tail End

The life line may end abruptly, it may form tassels, or it may just fizzle out. An abrupt ending suggests that the person will be strong and fit to the end of his days, while the other two scenarios signify failing health for some years before life comes to an end.

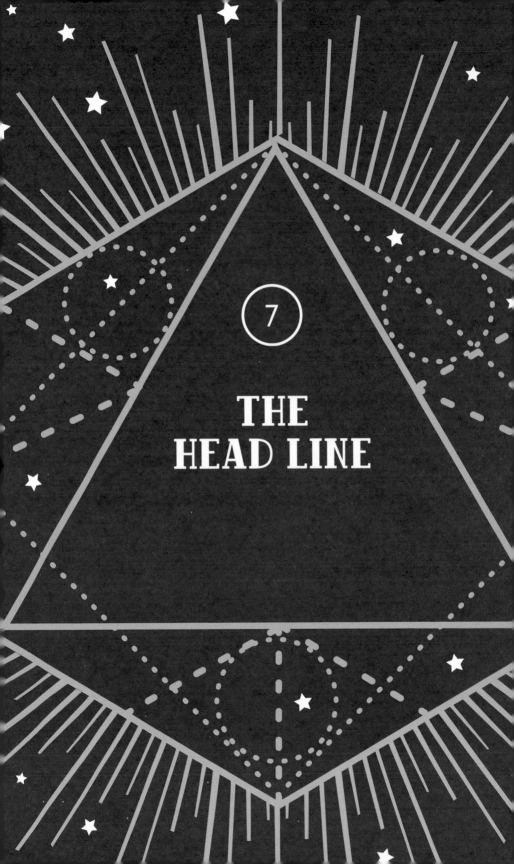

⑦

THE
HEAD LINE

The head line is associated with the way the mind works, and it often relates to education and the ability to earn money, the career, and to some extent, hobbies and interests. The head line starts on the thumb side of the hand and travels more or less across the hand, but the beginning and end can vary greatly. When the life line is weak but the head line is strong, there is more chance of overcoming bad health than otherwise.

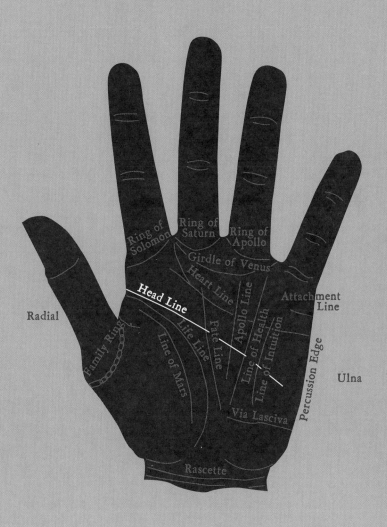

The Start of the Line

A Tied Head Line

A person with a head line that is tied to the life line for some part of its journey will be influenced by their parents, background, history, and culture, and this might be a very good thing. On the other hand, if the individual left home fairly early to escape a dysfunctional family, the parents' voices might continue to echo inside his head.

Sometimes there is a tragedy in the family that makes it hard for the subject to get away, but there might be a title, a stately home, a family farm, a big business, or some other kind of dynastic situation that keeps the subject back. Sometimes it is his early schooling or even a stint in the armed forces that leaves an impression, but it could also be a war situation or some other trauma that remains in his consciousness. Whatever the cause, it takes the person a long time to put it behind him and move on.

A Free Head Line

This person is optimistic, outward looking, and has the courage to make his own way. He may leave the neighborhood for good, or he may choose to remain close to his family because he's happy that way. His parents and family give him validation and encouragement, whatever road he chooses to tread.

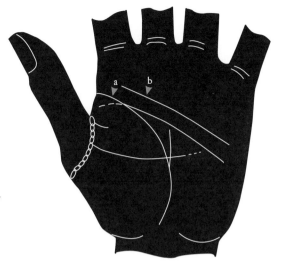

Tied (a) and Free (b) Head Lines

A Cat's Cradle

If the area between the head and life line, where they part company, looks muddled like the old child's game of cat's cradle that often shows that the subject hated school. Alternatively, school life represented an escape from a repressive family situation.

Cat's Cradle

The Shape of the Line

Straight

There is an old saying that a straight head line represents a mathematician and a curved line relates to an artist. There is something to be said for this, but, alternatively, a straight-lined person may go into politics.

A straight line that travels across the hand belongs to someone with a practical, logical mind who strives for success. He has an aptitude for mathematics, information technology, and science. Success in business really needs at least some downward slope to the line, because imagination and creativity play a part.

Sloping

A line that slopes gently downward belongs to someone with a creative imagination. This subject can succeed in business because he can pool his practical, creative, and imaginative skills and introduce a useful touch of intuition.

Straight (a) and Sloping (b)

Long

A long head line signifies a person who never stops learning. If the line is straight, the person may confine his studies to his career, while if it slopes or curves, his tastes will be more diverse. If the line reaches the percussion or if it touches other lines that do, this person may travel in connection with business or have business connections in other countries.

Long and Sloping

A curved or sloping head line that leans down toward the mount of Luna suggests imagination and creativity. If the line is long, the subject is discriminating and possibly a perfectionist. A curved long line endows a romantic and otherworldly kind of imagination and creativity, but also sensitivity, moodiness, depression, and sometimes a fearful nature. Some of this nervousness may be left behind from childhood experiences, but sometimes the subject is simply oversensitive. The individual might be a poet, artist, creative craft worker, musician, dancer, and so on.

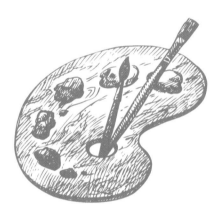

Short and Straight

When the line is straight and short, the subject is likely to be an expert on a particular subject. It is difficult to give a reading to this kind of person because they will only understand what you tell them in black-and-white terms or in terms of their special subject. Alternately, the individual may never bother to use his brain at all.

A short line that travels straight across the hand and suddenly plunges downward indicates a quick temper and sarcasm.

Farther Down the Line

It is common to see lines that tick or rise up from the head line, and this foretells times when the subject will do his best to overcome problems. A small rising line about three-quarters of the way along the line shows financial hardship and an effort to put this right.

A head line that bends upward or throws a line upward shows that there is an improvement in the person's life, probably due to career or financial improvements. He makes an effort to overcome his problems. Downward bends and falling lines can indicate losses, but they also predict jobs or interests that fall away from the person's life.

Upward Line

SIMIAN LINE

Some people don't have a separate heart and head line, but a single line stretching across the hand. This is known as a *simian line*. The word *simian* means "monkey," as it was once believed that monkeys had conjoined head and heart lines. This isn't so. I have studied these animals and even taken hand prints from a young ape.

If there are partial heart and head lines with some part of the lines being joined, this can make a person overly emotional and liable to go overboard when something excites or upsets him, and his judgment may be impaired. He can be intelligent and pleasant company, but his mind and his feelings are closely mixed.

Doubled Lines

A line can start as a single line and split into two, especially on the major hand. This shows a splitting of the person's energies, and it suggests the individual has two different kinds of jobs or interests. If the new line is above the original one, it shows stupendous efforts to improve the individual's career or financial circumstances.

A truly double head line, with two distinct starting and ending points, is a very unusual feature. The person may simply have a secondary interest, job, or hobby that he turns to from time to time, such an engineer who is also a champion tennis player or wonderful artist.

Disturbances on the Head Line

Islands

Islands on the head line are common. An isolated island indicates a career or educational setback, or maybe a financial setback or unhappiness at work. If the island forms a triangle or diamond, it tells us that the person has or will spend some time in prison! It can also result from a feeling of being imprisoned, possibly due to being in the wrong relationship. A really deep island that splits the head line into two for part of its journey can denote severe worry, stress, or even mental illness. Any jagged shape here is a warning that something is wrong, and it could represent a trauma to the head, a tumor, epilepsy, or something similar. A chain of small islands means that the subject suffers from headaches.

My friend and fellow palmist Beleta Greenaway told me that if the islands are pale in color, there are eye problems that come and go, but if the islands are pink or reddish, there is a real problem in connection with the eyes. An isolated island under the mount of Apollo also denotes an eye problem. Under Saturn, it indicates a hearing problem.

Forks

A fork on the head line is called the *writer's fork*, and it is said to show a talent for oratory or writing. Forks also imply versatility and varied interests. A subject with two different jobs or a career and an absorbing hobby can display such forks. This is another instance where the person does something ordinary for a living, but also does something expressive or artistic in his spare time.

Breaks

Breaks in the head line are common, and they may show time away from work due to sickness, especially if the ailment has something to do with the head. If there is a break with a square mark in it, the subject will recover.

Forks on the Head Line

Interference Lines

Long lines that wander across the hand and cut across the head line in an upward direction show some kind of interference or unpleasantness, and this can amount to bullying. If these come from inside the life line, family or in-laws are to blame. Short bars indicate short, sharp setbacks.

Tassels and Numerous Disturbances

Many small forks, branches, tassels, islands, breaks, and other disturbances are an indication of a troubled mind or of a lifetime of struggle. If the head line is in pieces, it is hard for the subject to get his act together. A tassel ending is not a good omen, as it points to the possibility of developing Parkinson's disease, Alzheimer's disease, or dementia in later life, but it can also indicate a lack of potassium or calcium.

❋ ❋ ❋

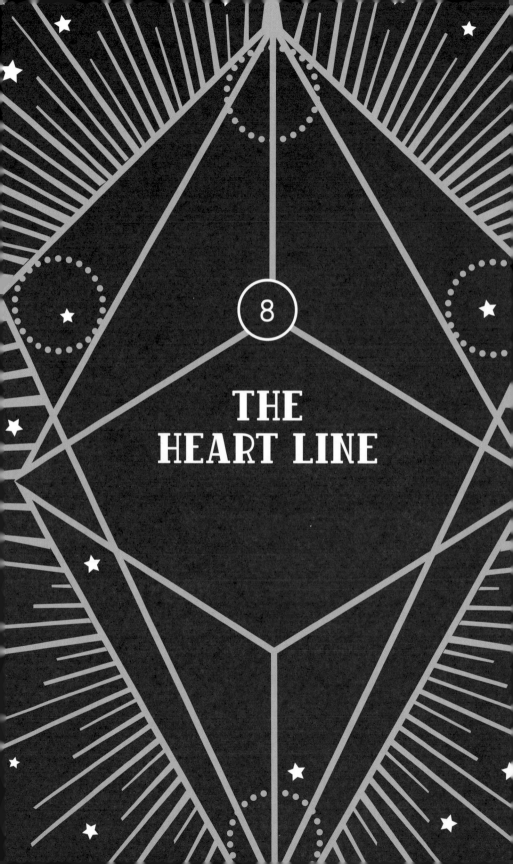

8

THE
HEART LINE

It would be nice if this line showed the progress of a person's love life in detail, because this is what the majority of people want to know, but unfortunately the heart line only offers tantalizing glimpses. Like all the other lines, it also gives some information about one's health, but overall it concerns the way the person loves and gives information about his relationships. It makes no difference about the person's sexuality, as feelings are the same for everyone, regardless of how or to whom they express them.

A person with a firm, clear heart line may be extremely lucky in love. He may, however, take his self-worth for granted, because he receives plenty of love and attention from his parents and others. He may be good-looking, wealthy, and have a charming outer personality.

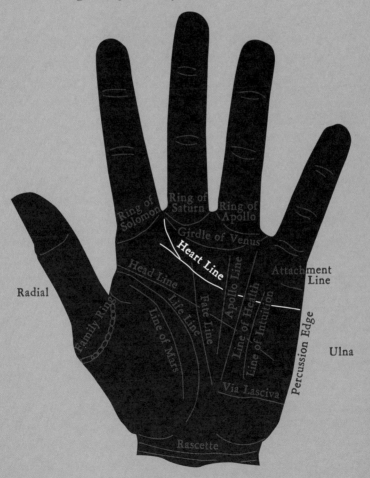

The Starting Point

I have always taken the percussion edge of the line as its starting point, but there are palmists who read the line starting from the other end. As it happens, it is difficult to time events on this line, so it doesn't matter that much either way.

The Shape of the Line

Long Line

A long heart line shows a capacity for affection and friendship, and an ability to empathize.

Short Line

This person may be selfish or unreasonable. He may be so focused on himself and his own problems that he can't take an interest in anyone else. I have also found short lines on the hands of those who are more interested in alcohol than in other people.

Curved Line

A curved heart line shows a capacity for affection and love, and the subject probably loves children, animals, and his family. When the line is long and curved, the subject is likely to fall in love with someone who understands him and who feels right for him. Parental approval or other considerations don't come into the picture, because this subject will follow his heart. This is the sign of a romantic person who is capable of falling deeply in love.

Straight Line

A straight heart line might cross the hand without bending upward, and it may end on or near the mount of Jupiter. This subject uses calculation when choosing a partner. He may select one from the right class, religion, financial bracket, or who has the right looks. He can love, but only up to a point, as falling deeply into romantic love isn't in his nature.

Women with a straight line will choose a potential lover who fits their religion, beliefs, or values. They may choose a man who is rich, has a particular kind of house or business, or who drives the right car. He may need to be a certain height, have the right hair color, or there could be a myriad of other considerations. Oddly enough, this kind of partnership can work as long as there is friendship, good intensions, shared values, and aspirations.

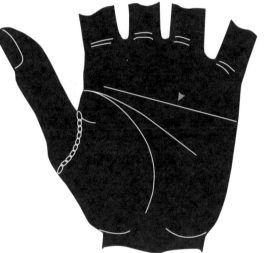

This line bodes well for businsess partnerships, friendships, neighborly relationships, and other non-love connections.

Shallow Line

A shallow heart line belongs to someone who wants to be loved but never quite manages to keep the interest of a partner. Sometimes selfishness or an inclination to argue over the slightest thing gets in the way. In other cases, the individual has addictive tendencies and his need for alcohol or drugs takes precedence over the needs and wishes of a partner.

Deep Line

A line that curves so deeply that it is actually close to the head line can be a sign of intolerance. This person may be a perfectionist who is full of rules and regulations about how life should be lived, and this translates into criticism or the imposition of impossible standards upon a partner. If this subject relaxes and puts his rule book away, he can be successful in love.

Disturbances on the Heart Line

Young people can have a flaky or disturbed line that settles down as they grow older. Sometimes you see this on adult hands, and in those cases, the effect is the result of a shortage of potassium or other dietary or hormonal problems. A shortage of potassium can cause depression, so this is worth asking subject about.

A Broken or Fragmented Line

An obvious break in the line shows heartbreak. A line that is in pieces belongs to someone who is fun and good company as a friend but probably hard to live with. This person can be very successful in his career but is perhaps tough and argumentative. If the line is broken below the gap between the mounts of Mercury and Apollo, the subject is celibate.

Broken Heart Line

Islands

Islands in the line indicate times of emotional trouble. Sometimes a clear island under the Apollo finger talks of a relationship that comes to a sudden end, and in a way that gives the subject a shock. In some cases this is due to the unexpected death of a partner, and in others it occurs because the partner walks out unexpectedly.

Breaks are often followed by a new piece of line, although this may be displaced above, below, or somewhat diagonal to the original line. Any fresh piece of line signifies a new way of thinking and, in some cases, a new relationship. Even if the line is a mess, a new piece of line reaching upward toward the fingers, shows that the person will find love later in life.

A Lack of Communication

A slanted line that links the heart and head lines suggests yunication or understanding between the partners.

Health Issues

Islands on the heart line can indicate problems with one's eyes, teeth, lungs, breasts, or many other conditions. Any serious disturbance on an otherwise fairly clear line suggests health problems in the chest, heart, or lung area.

A spiky, tasseled, or messy start to the heart line (the percussion end) indicates problems with the myocardium or arteries (also check the color of the nails and fingers as these may be pale or slightly blue). Blue pits on the line in the areas below and between Saturn and Mercury can indicate lung problems. A break in the line between where it bends up under the area between Saturn and Jupiter can indicate breast problems or something radically wrong with the lungs.

Partial Lines

Sometimes there is no real heart line. There may be a partial line at the start that then fizzles out; this suggests that a relationship never really got off the ground. As long as there is some new piece of line at the opposite end to the percussion, there is hope that the subject will be happy later on. If there is a line in the middle but not at the start or finish, the road to true love will be rocky, but this line also signifies a kind heart and a good sense of humor.

Friendship Lines

We see love in terms of romantic and sexual love, passion, soul mates, and mating or "partnering," which is the modern equivalent of marriage. There are, however, many forms of love that don't involve sex, including the love of one's parents, children, friends, and pets. A strong-looking line shows a capacity for those kinds of love as well as the sexual kind. The illustration below shows someone with a capacity for love, compassion, and friendship.

A person with a straight heart line that curves downward or that throws a heavy line downward toward the start of the head and life line shows a connection to the past and to his parents in some way. This may be due to very good or very bad childhood experiences, but the end result is that the past impinges on the present and the future.

Many people have light lines that fork and fall downward from the latter stages of the heart line, and these predict friendships.

Doubled Heart Line

Sometimes there are two heart lines, and these show a pleasant nature and a capacity for love and friendship. If there are a series of small heart lines, the person does his best to help humanity or save the planet or works for some kind of cause. He earns a lot of karmic benefits. This is a good person, but he may be unrealistic, impractical, and hopeless with money.

Flirtatiousness

Short lines that curve upward from the heart line are the sign of a flirt.

Simian Line

Some people don't have a separate heart and head line, but instead have one line that stretches across the hand. This is known as a *simian line.*

✳ ✳ ✳

9

THE FATE LINE

Some modern palmists call the fate line the *Saturn line*, on the basis that it wends its way toward the Saturn finger. Regardless of what you call it, the line determines the fate of a person in so many ways.

To my mind, this is the most important line on the hand because it shows what has happened, what is happening, and what is likely to happen in a person's life. But it isn't an easy one to decipher. In theory, the fate line runs from the lower part of the palm to the top of the hand, and it can do just that if the individual is so ambitious that nothing will stop him from reaching his goal.

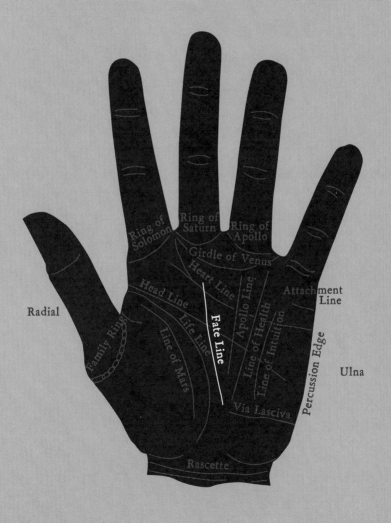

The line may not appear on the hand at all, or it can be so faint as to be scarcely visible. This subject lives an ordinary and mundane life without being particularly bothered about what other people think, making money, moving up in life, or anything other than taking things as easily as possible.

Sometimes the line starts early and peters out, suggesting that the person works hard early in life and is able to take things easy from middle age onward. Sometimes it doesn't start until halfway up the hand, suggesting the person didn't do much when he was young but gets into gear later on.

The Start of the Fate Line

Take a ruler and lay it across the width of the hand, from the knuckle at the base of the thumb to the percussion, and look at the area below this. Then look to see if there is a fate line running upward above the ruler, heading in the general direction of the mount of Saturn.

If the fate line starts in the of the lower part of the hand, the person will start to make his own way in life early, and he will be self-motivated. If it starts inside, near, or is part of the life line at this point, the subject's family might hold him back. They may treat him as a child or tie him to the family's apron strings, preventing him from going his own way in life. He may be forced to work in the family's business or do things the way he is told to do them.

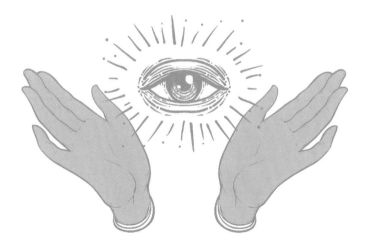

If the fate line starts near the life line, the family might have given him a good education and a good start in life and then allowed him to grow up. If the Jupiter finger is strong and long, this would emphasize that fact. Such a finger also shows strength of character, an independent nature, and the power to think independently.

If the line starts from the mount of Luna, the individual will receive help, understanding, and acceptance from friends and outsiders rather than from his family. There is a saying in Saint Luke's gospel that "no prophet is accepted in his own hometown," and that fits this particular scenario perfectly. The greater the distance from the life line, the earlier the person leaves home and does his own thing. This is even the case when the life and head lines are tied.

Lines That Enter the Fate Line

Lines that enter the fate line show people of importance coming into the person's life. This is often an indication of a marriage-type partnership, but it can represent any other important connection. Look at the length and relative depth or strength of the line to judge its importance.

The Fate Line

Lines Entering the Lower End of the Fate Line

The age at which something happens to a person is hard to judge on a hand, but anything in the lower zone is likely to occur before the age of twenty-three.

An entering line at the lower end of the hand suggests that the person is physically and mentally ready for a full relationship at a young age. Sexual experimentations and short-term friendships that include sex do not appear here, because this line doesn't usually show short-term matters. It talks more about important connections. If the person gets into a partnership at this time, the relationship could fail due to the subject's immaturity, but the usual situation is that the "entering line" denotes a full relationship starting at a relatively early age.

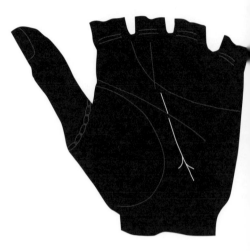

Lines Entering from the Radial Side

A line entering from the radial (thumb) side of the hand could be termed "marrying the girl next door," because it indicates meeting someone through one's family. It would be worth looking at the heart line in this case, because if it is straight rather than curved, this shows considerations other than, or in addition to, merely falling in love. A radially entering line could also indicate someone whom the subject meets at college or work. Either way, it talks about familiar territory.

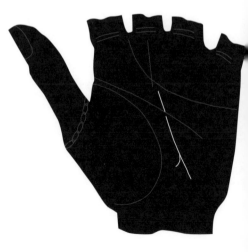

Lines Entering from the Ulna Side

Lines entering from the ulna (percussion) side of the hand talk about a partner who is chosen from somewhere outside the subject's usual territory, away from parents, school, and the workplace. It doesn't denote an unusual pairing, say of someone of a different background or religion, it just shows that the person is from the world outside.

A fine line entering from ulna might refer to an important friendship and help with one's career.

No Lines

A person can be in a relationship or even married with no lines entering the fate line, but the emotion won't be there. This could be a marriage of convenience or something that doesn't include love and feeling.

Lines Entering the Fate Line in the Middle or Upper Zone

A line entering the fate line midway or farther up the hand demonstrates people of influence coming into the person's life. These lines represent the appearance of lovers, partners, important work relationships, mentors, or anyone else of importance to the person. A long line shows an important connection of some kind.

Timing anything on the hand isn't easy to work out, but roughly speaking the fate line crosses the head line at around thirty-five, and it crosses the heart line at around fifty to fifty-five.

If you are giving a reading, be sure to tell the person that this isn't a reliable guide. Say what you think happened and when you think it happened, and ask your client to give you some feedback. Most people are happy to help.

Lines That Come and Go

Lines that enter, stay for a while, and then leave on the other side of the fate line show that someone comes into the individual's life, stays around for a while, and then drifts away again.

Two Fate Lines

This is another interesting one, as two lines that are closely parallel talk of a person taking the wrong road in life and living with regret. Sometimes there is a long spell of resentment or bitterness, which constitutes a waste of emotional energy and a waste of time.

Disturbances on the Fate Line

Remember, it's worth looking at both hands, because the minor hand often shows the depth of emotion expended on a problem in a way that the dominant hand does not.

A Diagonal Crossing Line

If there is a line that seems to join the heart and head line in a diagonal direction while also crossing the fate line, the person will have a relationship that comes to an end without the subject really knowing why. There is a lack of real communication and understanding between the couple.

Islands

Palmistry folklore says that islands on any line split and weaken the energy of the line. They relate to a period of difficulty, which in the case of the fate line can refer to almost any area of life. It can indicate a career problem, money difficulties, or something that goes wrong in the subject's love life.

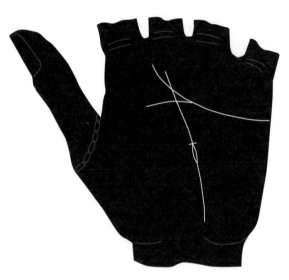

An accident that causes a health problem is possible, or the person might find it hard to continue with his spiritual development. In short, islands register aggravation of one kind or another. They are extremely common, and it would be a rare hand that doesn't have any on the fate line.

Islands can be short and oblong in shape, or they can form a long and narrow split that runs a fair distance up the line. Needless to say, the island gives you a clue as to the nature and length of the problem. If the island is short, fat, and obvious, the difficult period will be short and sharp, but it will be memorable. A long, narrow island or split in the fate line shows a long period of dissatisfaction.

Bars

A bar can be caused by someone interfering in the person's life or it can refer to an unexpected event. A short, heavily marked bar is unusual, but when seen, it predicts a full stop in the person's life. The cause of the problem could be practically anything, so look for a setback in the career path, financial shock, health problem, sudden marriage breakdown, or for someone causing a major problem to the subject. The main thing to remember is that this is a sudden, unexpected event rather than a long, drawn-out period of trouble.

Interference Lines

If a member of the family or an in-law interferes in the individual's life, a long line will snake out from the mount of Venus and cut across the fate line. This kind of intrusion upsets the person badly, and it can disturb his relationships and deflate his self-confidence. It is quite a common feature, and some unfortunate people have a number of these lines on their hands. Check to see whether the line also disturbs the head line, as this would affect the person's ability to think straight or work well. If it heads for the heart line or the attachment lines (see page 116) it could destroy a marriage.

In a way, this kind of line gives you a clue as to the nature of the person, because someone with a powerful sense of self-worth won't have any interference lines.

Breaks in the Line

A break in the fate line suggests a halt in the person's progress. He may stop work for a while or a woman may give up a career to have a baby. There may be a business loss or some other loss of direction. Alternately, the individual might just take a sabbatical and choose to drift for a while.

A Blank Hand

····◆◆◆◆◆◆····

Sometimes a very blank hand with few lines and little or no fate line also talks of pressure or interference from others. This may explain the person's lack of initiative or achievement in that he may consider any effort to be worthless as it will only bring criticism down on his head.

A "Y" break

When the fate line suddenly forms a small Y shape and then ends—probably starting again farther up the hand—this means the person gets so fed up that he walks away from a situation. He may have been struggling with a career or a business, only to realize that he is sick and tired of it. This may lead him to resign and then take a completely different direction. Another scenario is the subject waking up one day and realizing that he is never going to be happy in his marriage, so he takes a hike.

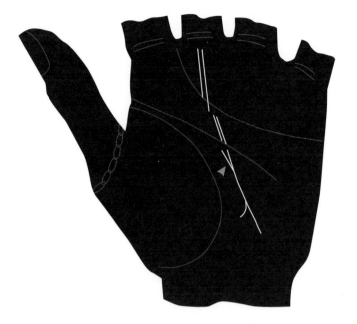

A Y break always reminds me of the story I heard about a guy who had a high-powered job and an ungrateful, critical, misery for a wife. One day he up and went to New Zealand, because this put the maximum possible distance between his job and his wife, and him. Later on, he started a business supplying plants (the green, growing kind, not industrial installations) to large offices, and going around watering and feeding the plants thereafter. He didn't make much money, but he was happy.

Supporting Lines

You'll often see an area where many short lines gather together on either side of the fate line looking rather like a fence that is made from a row of posts. Sometimes this phenomenon extends across the hand and forms an "energy rhythm," but sometimes it just surrounds the fate line. These lines point to a busy period where the person is fulfilling a number of different functions. If there is a break in the fate line or a Y split followed by a break, and then a new line starts with lots of these little lines running parallel on both sides of it, it's likely that the person's career ends and he starts his own business.

Advice on Reading the Fate Line

When judging the fate line, see how it changes direction, how it deepens or becomes shallow. Look at what crosses it, breaks it, interferes with it, or supports it. Read it as though you were looking at a road that wends its way across the countryside.

THE
APOLLO
LINE

10

I call this the Apollo line, but some modern palmists call it the sun line. The Apollo line runs up the hand toward the Apollo finger in the same way that the fate line travels toward the Saturn finger. Often the Apollo line is fragmentary, but there are usually some line parts on the middle and upper sections of the hand under the Apollo finger. There are several meanings to this line, but it is always a positive influence.

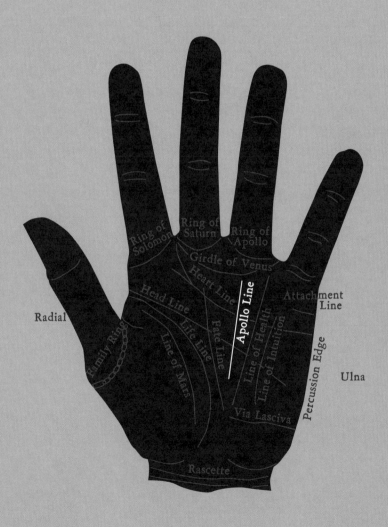

The Condition of the Line

Even if the line isn't complete, if there is a fair bit of it and it is nice and clear, it points to success and achievement and even potential fame and fortune. The individual is strong, capable, and doesn't give up easily, so he follows his dream and it leads to success.

Other effects of this line are an interest in music, the arts, decor, design, and creativity of all kinds. A nice, clear Apollo line also denotes setting up a home relatively early in life and generally enjoying family and domestic life. Another outcome for a well-defined line is one of happiness and taking joy in little things such as the wilderness, flowers, a nice view, tuneful melodies, good weather, and much else of a gentle nature.

An Early Line That Fizzles Out

Sometimes you see a line coming up from the lower end of the hand but fading out at some point. This shows that the individual may have been into art, design, music, and so on as a youngster but put these dreams aside when the need to be practical and earn money took over. Sometimes these interests re-emerge later in life when the person retires. In this case, check for a fresh bit of line running upward on the mount of Apollo.

A Late-Starting Apollo Line

Many hands only start to show an Apollo line about halfway up, which suggests it will take time for the person to settle into a home he likes, and it also indicates that an interest in and enjoyment of artistic or creative matters starts in early middle age.

A Fragmented Apollo Line

The Apollo line can form all kinds of bits and pieces, and this can relate to house moves, changes of location, and changes in a person's creative or musical interests. Sometimes a line that runs alongside the Apollo line talks about two homes or a home and a trailer. Check for confirmation by looking at the property ring that runs round the base of the thumb.

No Apollo Line

The subject may not be into creativity, music, or arty matters, and he may never have a settled home.

Lines on the Mount of Apollo

Old-time palmists used to say that if there is one, two, or several lines running up the mount of Apollo toward the Apollo finger, the person will be happy when he is old. He should find himself living where he wants to be, and he should have creative hobbies that keep him amused.

A Location That Is Dictated by Circumstances

A line somewhere on the Apollo mount but sitting close to the mount of Saturn suggests that the individual will live in a particular place due to circumstances rather than by choice.

Lines between the Apollo and Saturn Mounts

V-Split on the Apollo Line

Looking After Others

A long, fine line that splits into a long V rising up the Apollo mount shows that the person will look after someone else when he gets older. He may care for his parents, in-laws, or others when they can't care for themselves. The aged invalid may not live with the person, but he will take responsibility for seeing that the person is all right.

When my much-loved mother-in-law was in her nineties, we put her into a really nice nursing home close to where we live. She was happy there, she made friends with other residents, and she enjoyed musical and entertaining evenings. She attended mass each week, and she made friends with a nun who liked to call in on her. We visited her on a regular basis, and it was a pleasure for us to do so. My husband and I both developed the V-shaped mark on our Apollo mounts at that time, but when my mother-in-law eventually died, our lines started to fade, and they eventually vanished from both our hands.

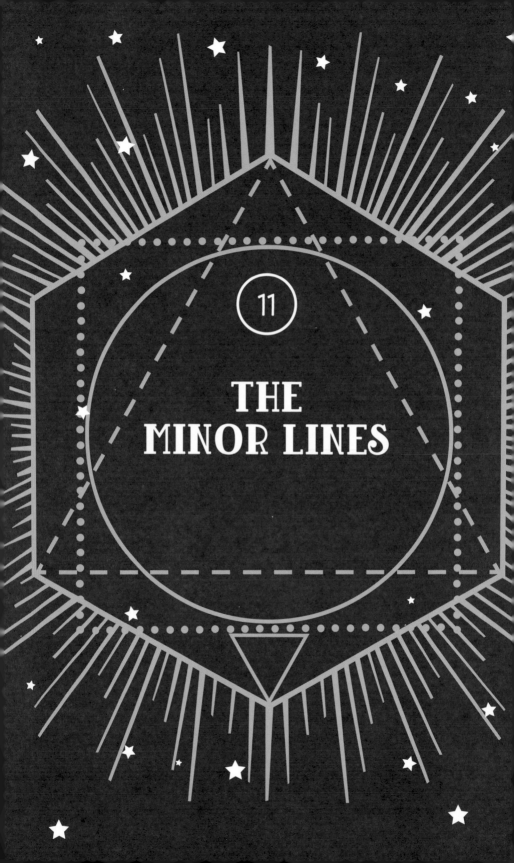

11

THE MINOR LINES

There are many types of minor lines, and most hands have a few but not all of them. There are also often stray lines that are individual to each person. Please bear in mind that lines can change over time, and some of the minor ones come and go quite quickly. It is worth taking prints of the hands from time to time, so you can keep track of what changes.

The Length of Life

Some people want to know how long they will live, and while it isn't given to us to know the whole story, the following will supply some information. Please be careful how and to whom you give this kind of information.

If there are lines rising to the top of the hand on most of the mounts, the person will live a long life. The lines don't have to be particularly heavy, but they should be present. If there are no lines, it may be that the hand is the type

A READING TO REMEMBER

It isn't often that a palmist gets the opportunity to knock the socks off a client, but it's wonderful when it happens. One day, I noticed a deeply scored travel line on the client's hand coming in from the percussion around the head line area, so I asked the lady if she'd recently paid an important visit to Canada. She agreed that she had visited family in that country.

When I peered at the line, I saw a small line rising straight up from the middle and slightly to the right of the center of the travel line. I chanced it and asked if she had been to Toronto, this being a large city somewhat to the right of the middle of Canada. She agreed that she had. I then saw an even finer line rising up from the travel line, so I decided to have some fun. I asked the client if her journey had taken her to Yonge Street—knowing that Yonge Street runs north/south through the middle of the city. She looked at me in utter amazement.

I was pretty amazed myself by this time, but knowing Toronto as I do, I decided to press my luck even further. I brought out my magnifying glass and stared at the little line, noticing a small branch somewhat less than a quarter of the way up sticking out of the tiny rising line and pointing to the right, like a side street running off a main road. I told her that the place she had visited was a little to the north of the Eaton Centre but on the other side of the road, and it was a turning off Yonge Street. I went on to say that it was past the shoe-mending and key-cutting shops, but I couldn't tell her the name of the street as the map of the hand didn't show names, only places. I apologized for the fact that this was as near as I could get. To my utter amazement (much more than hers, I suspect) I'd gotten it absolutely right!

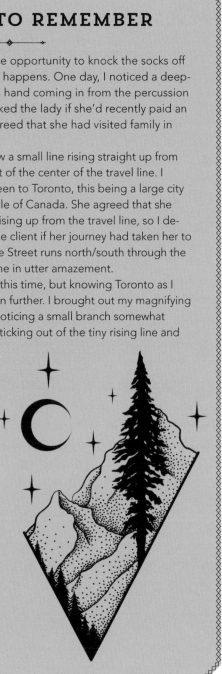

that is particularly clear of lines, or it may be that the person needs to improve his health in order to reach an old age. Lines come and go, so changes in lifestyle on the part of the person will be reflected in his hands.

Travel Lines

Lines that enter the hand from the percussion relate to important journeys, time spent overseas, or even business or family connections in other countries. The rule isn't hard and fast, but roughly speaking, Europe figures in the area between the heart line and the head line, North America sits around the end of the head line, and Asia and the Middle East lie along the Mars area of the percussion. Australia, New Zealand, South Africa, and South America fall into place down the side of Luna.

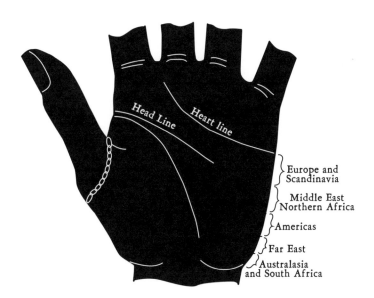

The Allergy Line

This enters the mount of Luna from the percussion side of the hand. Some palmists call this the *via lasciva* and others the *via lascivia*. This small line is traditionally said to register intolerance or allergies to certain foods or materials. This does seem to be born out in reality, although the reactions aren't particularly severe.

Property Lines

This line runs round the base of the thumb, and old-time palmists call this the *family ring*, but it seems to refer to property, so I call it the *property ring*. Sometimes there is one clear line, but it can look more like a chain or flaky line, or it can amount to a number of partial lines. This seems to say something about the property that a person owns or rents and the location in which he lives.

If the line is long and clear, the person tends to stay in one place for a long time, perhaps only moving two or three times in his life. If it is muddled and bitty, there will be lots of moves and little real attachment to a particular property or area.

If there is more than one line, there will be more than one property in the person's life at once, and this could represent a main home and a vacation home, or even a trailer that the individual uses for his vacation.

Lines Parallel to the Life Line

Lines that run inside or outside the life line can be called *Mars lines*, *median lines*, *companion lines*, or *shadow lines*. They add strength to the person when they need it, possibly during a period of illness or unhappiness. They can also represent spiritual guides or relatives on "the other side" who give love and support to the subject.

The Health Line

Some people call this line the *Mercury line*, because it runs upward from the lower part of the palm toward the mount of Mercury. In some cases there is more than one line, and some palmists call one line the *health line* and the secondary one that is nearer to the center of the palm the *Mercury line*. Having said this, I would read the stronger of the two lines as the health line.

If the health line is clear of lines and looks strong, the person is in good health. A strong, straight line, however, also suggests an interest in health and healing and possibly a career in the field of health. This applies to both conventional medicine and complementary therapies. This line is often flaky and fragmented, as we all go through periods of bad health from time to time.

Disturbances on the Health Line

Breaks in the health line suggest times of weakness. Flakes falling off suggest nutritional deficiencies, and pits denote a severe problem at the time of the reading, but these go away once the person recovers.

Healing Lines

Healing lines, or *healing striate* as some palmists call them, are three small, more or less vertical lines on the mount of Mercury. These can crown the health line, or the health line can be detached from these lines. Sometimes the lines are crossed by a diagonal line.

These lines show that the subject has some interest in healing, and that he may work in a health field. This could be the medical world or the dental one, as an osteopath, podiatrist, optician, veternarian, or any number of health-related careers. Equally, he may work as a complementary therapist or spiritual healer.

Lines Coming Up from the Heart Line

A bunch of little lines under the mount of Mercury that resemble a plant sprouting up from the heart line shows that the subject works for the benefit of the public. He may be a social worker, a retail clerk, a palmist, or frankly anything else that helps people.

Teaching Line

If one of the healing lines reaches up to the inside of the Mercury finger, the person is a natural teacher.

Curve of Intuition

Some people have a curved
line on the percussion side
of the hand. This line can
be long and curved or short
and curved. It may appear in
place of the health lines or
run alongside it. This line is
seen on the hands of those
who are intuitive and maybe
even psychic. It is a sign of
sensitivity to the feelings
of others and to one's own
feelings.

Rings Under the Fingers

Ring of Solomon

A vaguely ring-shaped line can
occur under any finger, but the
most common is a ring or even
a diagonal line under the Jupiter
finger, which is called the *ring
of Solomon.* This shows that the
subject can be a good friend or
a teacher. He likes to help and
counsel others, so he might
work as a psychotherapist or
even a palmist, or he may just
be a good person to go to in
times of trouble.

Ring of Saturn

This ring is unusual, but it belongs to a person who may be too timid for relationships or someone who is a loner.

Ring of Apollo

This ring is often partial. It lies below the Apollo finger and it means that there is some kind of wedge or wall between the person and his family. Alternatively, there could be a blockage to creativity.

Spinster Line, aka Widow's Line

When a line surrounds the Mercury finger in an unbroken pattern, the subject doesn't stay with anyone for long, and he may never settle into a relationship. He may lose partners through death, hence the name *widow's line*.

Spiritual Growth Line

A line that reaches up into the gap between Mercury and Apollo suggests spiritual development. If light shows through the fingers when they are closed up, the person might be subject to unknown or spooky forces!

Companion Lines

Two small parallel lines
reaching between the
Apollo finger and the
Saturn finger predict that
the person won't be alone
in this life. If the lines
converge, the relationship
will be a full marriage-type
partnership, and it might
even continue into a future
incarnation.

Trident under Apollo

A three-line trident under the Apollo finger suggests that the individual will
always be able to find money in times of hardship or figure out a solution to a
problem before it's too late. If the area is blank, this suggests something wrong
with the subject's home and family life, or even that he has no home or family
life to speak of.

Military Marks

Little lines on a puffed up mount between the start of the life line and the
thumb suggest a life in the military or a fondness for military or quasi-military
services such as the scouts. This person might come from a military family or
be in love with someone in the armed forces.

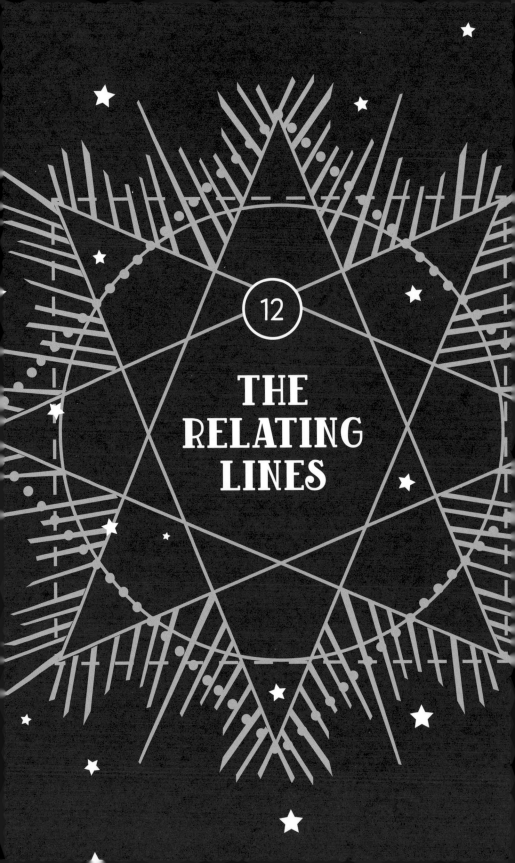

12

THE
RELATING
LINES

Take Care

Young women are often keen to hear about love and relationships, and many want to know whether they will have children. We can tell people what *should* happen according to the marks and lines on their hands, but real life is a combination of fate, free will, and circumstances—and everything can change over time. When a person changes his or her mind, the lines on the hand can also change, so take care when giving information and never be too absolute.

Anyway, this is what *should* happen in terms of relating lines . . .

Relationships Coming into the Person's Life

As we have already seen in the chapter on the fate line, lines that join the fate line show important people coming into an individual's life. These might be important romantic partners, but they could equally be mentors, work colleagues, friends, neighbors, or other (hopefully) beneficial influences. If the line joins the fate line for a while and then exits on the other side, the connection breaks and the other person drifts away.

Attachment Lines

Attachment lines come into the hand from the percussion side onto the mount of Mercury, between the heart line and the bottom of the Mercury finger. Gently rubbing a little talcum powder into the area will make the lines easier to see.

These little lines used to be called *marriage lines*, but these days they refer to important relationships, as the hands pick up on *emotional* attachments rather than marriage certificates. They can concern any adult relationship that involves love and emotion. The lines work in the same way for everyone whatever the sexual orientation. Note: You may find the minor hand more accurate when reading these lines, as it connects more to feelings and emotions than to the world outside and career success.

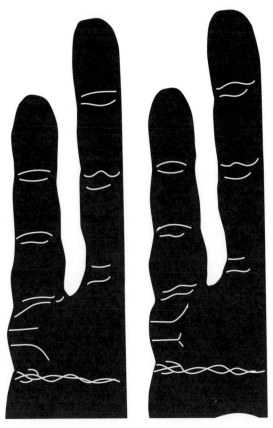

Attachment Lines

One Strong Line

The theory is that one strong line
means one lasting attachment, but in
my experience it can mean the desire for
one strong partnership and a tendency
to work at any relationship. If a partner
leaves or dies, the subject might eventually
go on to form another relationship,
and he will be just as serious about the
subsequent one as he was about the first.

Two Lines

A couple of lines suggest that the person
will have more than one important
relationship during his lifetime. If the first
partnership isn't a happy one, the subject
will question it and eventually call it off.
Sooner or later, he will find a new lover.

One Strong Attachment Line

Several Lines

You sometimes see a number of fine lines, and this may suggest that the person
likes his freedom. He is unlikely to settle into a permanent relationship with any
one person. If the girdle of Venus has a line reaching to the mount of Mercury,
the person won't want a permanent relationship.

Another common scenario here is of someone who is young and not really
ready for a full commitment, or perhaps someone playing the field while
between partnerships. When he makes up his mind to settle down, most of the
fine lines will fade away, leaving one or two strong ones behind.

Strong Lines and a Few Faint Lines

This kind of thing is often visible on the hand of a middle-aged or older person
who has done his share of living. One or two strong lines will refer to long-
term partnerships, while the fainter ones relate to people who were relatively
insignificant. Oddly enough, even a marriage can become unimportant in the long
run when compared to a passionate affair of the heart. Even if the relationship

Timing

····◆◆◆◆◆◆◆····

I have never read this or heard it anywhere else, but over the years I have noticed that a person's first major love relationship is shown by the attachment line closest to the heart line, with the next one above it, the one after above that one, and so on.

doesn't get as far the couple living together, it can leave a stronger impression than a weak marriage. It all comes down to the level of emotion stirred up by the relationship.

Strong Feelings

Check the percussion side of the hand, and if you see one line reaching toward the back of the hand, or two lines joining to become one, the person is very serious about his relationship. If there are two lines, he will try hard but if things become really unpleasant, he will leave and move on.

The Shape of the Attachment Lines

The shape of the lines shows the nature of the attachments. This can be surprisingly accurate while the event is still on the person's mind, but, over time, the lines can change or vanish. For instance, if someone breaks up with a partner, moves on, and spends many decades with a subsequent partner, the pain of the first relationship fades, and so does the line.

A LINE THAT CURVES DOWNWARD

This shows that the subject is being dominated or put upon by the partner, and it can lead him to walk away from the partnership.

A Downward-Curved Attachment Line

A Decision Line

A strange diagonal line can appear at the end of an attachment line, and it shows that the subject decides to bring the relationship to an end, and the end could come suddenly.

A Forked Attachment Line

FORKS

A line that ends in a sudden fork tells us that the subject puts up with a bad situation for a long time and then he suddenly calls it a day. When asked about it, he will say that he doesn't regret leaving and that he should have done so much sooner. A long fork shows that the partnership was never really fulfilled and the end was a long time coming.

When there are two very close lines in parallel, the partners live somewhat separate lives. A strong line with a faint one traveling beside it shows that the subject has something else going on in his life. This may be a secret lover, but it could be some other kind of absorbing interest. It is as though the individual is conducting his partnership on autopilot with his main focus elsewhere. If the main line curves up to Jupiter, it shows that the partnership leaves the subject sexually unfulfilled, and this could obviously lead to the individual looking elsewhere for satisfaction.

A LINE THAT CURVES UPWARD

In this case, the person himself is dedicated to the relationship, but his or her partner's attention is on other things. This could be a job, sports, a band, animals, or whatever. There may be a lot of money coming into the house, but the relationship is being allowed to wither.

If the line is straight but throws a small fork upward, the partner will still be successful, but it won't impact on the relationship in a bad way. In this case, both partners will benefit from the good income.

An Island on the Attachment Line

This talks about a partner who is ill or in some kind of difficulty. If the line straightens out after the island and continues on its way, the partner will recover.

Upward-Curved Attachment Line

The Girdle of Venus

The girdle of Venus curves under the Saturn and Apollo fingers and lies above the heart line. Old-fashioned palmistry books say this is a sign of a hysterical person who gets himself worked up over nothing. Some modern palmists, however, say it's a sign of sensitivity.

I have never found the girdle to signify hysterics, but someone with a full girdle is very in tune with his own feelings, and he may also be able to tune in to the feelings of others. He may have crushes on people when young, but he gets over these and doesn't give his heart easily when he is an adult. The subject may be psychic and able to sense spiritual energies, and he may be into spiritual or religious matters.

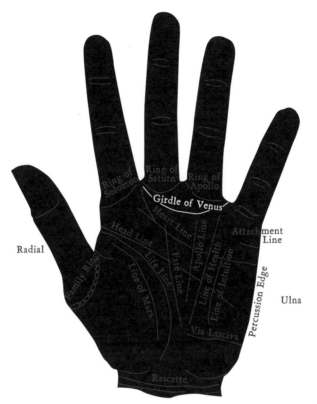

Full Girdle of Venus

Fragments of the Girdle of Venus

Fragments of the Girdle of Venus

Very few people have a full girdle, but many subjects have fragments. This adds a bit of useful sensitivity. The usual scenario is for there to be a fragment at either end of the girdle and a gap in the middle.

If a section of girdle reaches the mount of Jupiter or is between the Jupiter and Saturn fingers, and if the fate line blends into the girdle, the person will put business, politics, or career matters before his personal life. When a partial girdle is under the Saturn finger, it means the person needs security in love and financial matters.

When the partial girdle appears under the Apollo or Mercury finger, the subject will choose emotional fulfillment over career matters. He links to others on an intellectual level, and he falls in love with their minds. He may fall for a guru, a tutor, or someone who talks well and sounds knowledgeable and intelligent. Or he may fall for someone who understands him on a spiritual level. He needs to be with like-minded people, and if he marries young and finds that his partner doesn't share his interests, he will leave in favor of life among those who are on his wavelength.

Child Lines

Child lines run downward from the bottom of the Mercury finger and through the attachment lines. Like so much in palmistry, especially in the tricky area of love, relationships, and family members, the lines may not tell the entire truth. However, this is what should be the case . . .

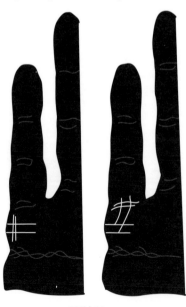

Child Lines

- No child lines or lines that don't cut through the attachment lines mean no children.
- One line indicates one child, two lines equal two children, and three lines show three children.
- More than three children are hard to define.
- Vertical lines usually refer to male children, while diagonal ones usually mean females.
- A line that splits into two and looks a bit like a catapult indicates twins.

• Lines that turn away to the side of the hand denote children who are keen to leave their parents as soon as possible.
• Broken lines may refer to a difficult relationship with the child or that something is wrong with the child.
• A line with an island shows a sick or injured child.
• Mangled lines show problems of one sort or another with the child.
• A very short, squiggly line that might be surrounded with a bluish color shows a miscarriage or termination.
• A red dot or pinprick hole on the attachment line below a child line also indicates the end of a pregnancy by miscarriage or termination. A small, blue vein may drift out of this crater.
• Many fine vertical lines or a grille denote a hysterectomy.
• A glassy glow, glassy warts, or a watery appearance here should be taken seriously as it can indicate cancer in the reproductive organs.

Sibling Lines

Sibling Lines

These lines form on the thumb side of the hand. They can be seen on the edge of the hand, below the Jupiter finger and above the heart line. They relate to siblings or those who feel like siblings, such as cousins, friends who one grew up with, and so on. These lines can stay on the hand for years and then fade away if the relationship ends. Read these in the same way you would the attachment lines.

❋ ❋ ❋

13

MARKS,
COLORS,
AND WARTS

Old-time and Romany palmists used to give more credence to marks found on the hand than modern palmists do. Some of their ideas were scary, such as the "hangman's cross" or the "cross of rescue from drowning." Today, marks are seen as useful for looking into short-term situations, because they fade once the circumstances improve. At the time of this writing, I have a gray mark next to the life line on my minor hand, and in this case, the life line represents the spine, so the mark signifies an injury to muscles, ligaments, and tendons near my spine, and this is a true and painful fact!

X Cross

Crosses

A cross is a ✝ or X formation

A Cross on Different Mounts

A cross on the mount of Jupiter brings a feeling of achievement, and it can also denote a talent for teaching. If the cross is near the end of the heart line, traditional palmistry says this predicts marrying into money.

The old-time palmists believed that a cross on the mount of Saturn was "the hangman's cross." It was a sign of disgrace and indicated one would be executed as a result of committing some terrible crime. The truth is that it warns of a career setback and perhaps a loss of status.

A cross on the mount of Apollo means gains that don't come as a direct result of work that is done at the time, which means the cross isn't connected with wages or a fee for doing a particular job. These crosses can concern royalties that drift in over the years or even a win on a lottery or in a raffle. Judge the size of the win or gain by the size and depth of the mark.

A cross on Mercury seems to indicate technical expertise such as working with computers or machinery, or having some kind of engineering or design talent. Look for Mercury and Apollo fingers that are longer than the Jupiter finger, as these will back up that finding.

The mystic cross is a cross that lies between the head and heart line, and it must stand alone. Some people believe fervently in the mystic cross as a sign of psychic gifts, while others don't believe it has any meaning at all. In my own experience, I've never found this mark to mean anything special.

Squares

Squares can appear on any part of the hand, but they often show up on the lines, sometimes surrounding a break, an island, or some other sign of difficulty. In those cases, it is a protective sign. For instance a person with a square over a break on any line depicts an illness or an accident from which the person recovers.

I once saw an elderly lady who had a large break on her head line, but it was covered by a square. I asked her what had happened, and she said that she'd fallen from a horse when she was a young woman and banged her head on a hard piece of ground. She had been expected to die, or at the very least to have severe brain damage, but she recovered fully and lived a perfectly normal life from then on.

Restriction

The less useful aspect of the square is that it causes restriction, and it can appear on any line or mount. For instance, a square on the heart line can be extremely frustrating, as it makes it hard for the subject to find love. He may need to look at his own behavior to see what he is doing to mess up his chances. Even when the square is helping someone to recover from sickness or an accident, it says that the person's life is on hold while he recovers.

A square on the head line can cause difficulty in career matters. If one appears on any mount, it slows down or restricts the activities connected to that mount.

Stars

In most cases, the star warns of a period of severe stress. It can register an unexpected event, which has a sudden and deep impact. A star on the mount of Apollo, however, can mean sudden fame and fortune.

Triangles

Triangles often appear attached to a line, and these represent times of frustration or confinement. Indeed, a triangle connected to and hanging below the head line can denote time spent in prison!

Talent

An isolated triangle on a mount suggests talent, likely in a sphere that is connected to that mount. As examples, the person could be high up in

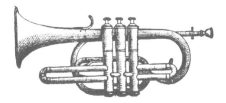

business if the triangle is on Mercury, a successful artist if it is on Apollo, a champion swimmer if it is on Luna, and so on.

Grilles

Grilles are hard to define as they often show up as muddy, pitted, and heavily marked areas that obscure some part of the hand. There are several meanings to these.

Illness and Operations

I have seen grilles appear at times when illness, an accident, or an operation causes a shock to the system. The specifics aren't easy to pinpoint, but if you imagine a figure lying on the hand with his head at the top and his feet at the bottom, the location of the grille will roughly correspond to the ailment. A grille of this nature will disappear when the person recovers.

Another theory is that a grille shows intensity in the person's character in relation to that area of the hand. For instance, a grille on Venus depicts someone who is extremely possessive, while a grille on Jupiter indicates someone who will do anything for success and money.

Dots

Dots can signify an illness, especially when seen on the health line, or they can indicate a period of unhappiness or depression, especially when on the head line. They disappear quickly once the person has recovered.

Chains

A chained line shows a lack of confidence or assertiveness, but chains on the head line show trouble with the eyesight. If the middle of each tiny island in the chain on the head line is red, the problem is permanent. If it is pale, the problem comes and goes.

The latter can correspond to a classic sign of diabetes in which the lenses in the eyes become cloudy when the subject's blood glucose level is too high, but when the level comes back under control, the lenses clear once again. I have this problem myself, and my own vision can be misty when I am tired and when my blood glucose level is too high. If this happens, it tells me that I must take more care with my food, drink lots of water, and do some exercise to clear the overload from my system.

Colors

Coloration of the hands is an important health indicator. I deal with this in more depth in the chapter on health, but in brief, if you see a small red patch somewhere, it shows that the person has recently suffered some kind of shock or bad news. See which area the patch is on and ask the subject what is going on. For instance, if on Venus, it might be something to do with money, property, or his love life. On Mars, he might be the victim of a bully or have a fight on his hands for some other reason. Also check the line the red patch is on or near.

Warts

Warts and verrucae are common in childhood, and they don't have any special meaning. If an adult has a nasty wart, it registers a blockage or a problem associated with the area of the hand on which it sits. If the wart is on the palmar side of the hand, the subject will be at least partially responsible for his own troubles, while on the back of the hand, the state of affairs is caused by someone other than the person himself. Surprisingly, this is a seriously bad sign, because it denotes a time of real trial and tribulation. Here is a sampling of wart problems:

- When on the Jupiter finger, something is impeding the subject's progress, and it may affect his feelings of self-worth.
- The Saturn finger is the most common place for a wart to appear, and when there, it affects the person's basic means of survival. Something may be stopping him from being able to provide for his family for a while.
- When on the Apollo finger, something is amiss in the individual's home and family life. There may be trouble connected to his children or his personal relationships. A creative project might be stalled.

THE BACK OF THE HAND

The back of the hand is like a mirror image of the front of the hand, so imagine a knitting needle piercing completely through hand to match the features on the palm to the back. Start by checking the backs of the fingers.

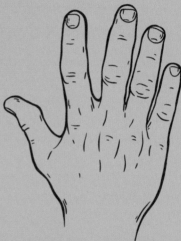

- A red patch on the back of the Jupiter finger means someone is trying to put the subject down or interfere in his progress at work.

- A red patch on the back of the Saturn finger threatens his basic security and the roof over his head.

- A red patch on the back of the Apollo finger might signal a health problem or something to do with the creative side of life.

- A red patch on the back of the Mercury finger might tell of a communication problem or an issue with machinery. Strangely enough, this may also indicate a temporary problem with a person's sex life.

- A patch on the back of the thumb means a blockage on any activity that allows the subject to move about, which might be anything from a strained ankle to his bus route being suspended. Alternatively, it can register a severe blow to the ego or someone stomping on the subject's ambitions and preventing him from getting anywhere.

- If on the Mercury finger, there is a serious communication problem. The subject may be living with someone who is a bully or who deliberately misunderstands him.
- If on the thumb, the individual is prevented from exerting his will, so he becomes frustrated and angry.
- When on the first phalange of any finger, there will be mental anguish.
- The person can't put his dreams and desires into action when the wart is on the middle phalange.
- When on the base phalange, there is financial hardship and a lack of security and support from others.
- A wart on the palm side of the hand reads in connection with the meaning of the line or mount on which it appears.

14

SKIN RIDGE PATTERNS

We're all familiar with fingerprints, and on TV shows such as *CSI*, we sometimes hear the actors mention loops, whorls, and arches to describe patterns found in the skin ridges on the palmar side of hands and fingers. This is true to life, because police forces everywhere have adopted the terminology that palmists use. When you think about it, the science of finger-printing is only about a hundred years old, while palmistry and its attendant terminology reach back thousands of years, so the police are wise to use terms that have been understood by so many for so long.

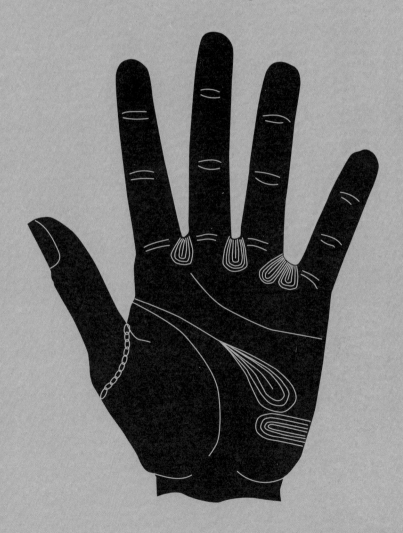

The palmar side of any hand is covered in skin ridges, but not everyone has loops, whorls, or peacock's eye formations on the palm. Interestingly, apes and monkeys are similar to us in this way. Their hands display all the usual lines, but they have many more loops and whorls than we do, and they have them on more parts of the hand than we do.

Different skin ridge patterns connote different things. Loops can occasionally form a peacock's eye in their middle, and this adds a touch of artistry and talent to the subject. A whorl is useful in some cases as it suggests a flair for something, but it can belong to someone who goes over the top about a favorite subject or their field of work to the point where they become boring.

The Rajah Loop

This loop appears on the space between the mounts of Jupiter and Saturn. It shows the subject has a "royal" connection, due to being descended from a royal family of some kind The roots of palmistry are in India where Rajahs are royalty, so the name of this loop makes perfect sense. A Rajah loop on one hand certainly shows a royal connection, but when they appear on both hands and are clearly marked, there is definitely blue blood somewhere in the person's background—and probably not that far back!

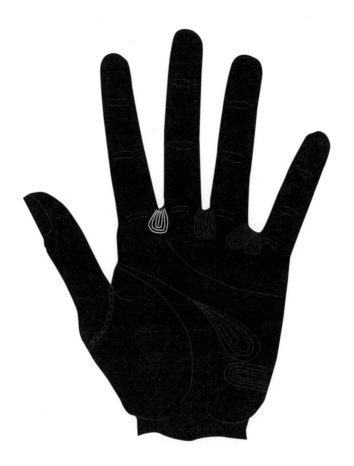

Many years ago, I was working at a psychic fair when two really good-looking young men sat down in front of me. Their accents and appearance told me they were European, and they were clearly brothers. Only one of them wanted his hands read, but as soon as I started, I couldn't help noticing two clearly marked Rajah loops. I told my client that he had royal blood in his veins, and I asked if I could check the hands of his brother. Brother number two promptly held out his hands, and sure enough the Rajah loops were both present. The first brother told me they were indeed "royal" as they were the dukes of Braganza, which was once the royal family of Portugal!

The Loop of Serious Intent

This loop is located between the mounts of Saturn and Apollo, and it shows a serious mind. The person reads deeply, he needs to understand things, and he learns throughout life. He is also a very hard worker.

Strings of Beads

When a skin ridge pattern breaks down into what looks like a string of beads, there is a serious health problem that may be caused by alcoholism or drug addiction.

The Loop of Humor

This loop sits between Apollo and Mercury and it shows not only a sense of humor, but also a love of words, writing, communicating, and so on. The subject may have a talent for foreign languages. When the mount is high and the loop prominent, the person loves pets and animals generally.

The Loop of Style

This loop can appear beside the loop of humor or it can be separate. The illustration is exaggerated here, as this loop twists to the side so that it is partially under the Apollo finger. On a real hand, it would go straight down from the gap between fingers. It can register vanity, but more likely it belongs to a chic and stylish person.

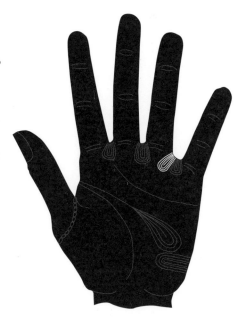

The Loop of Memory

This endows the owner with a good memory. It is handy for professions like sales and teaching where the person needs to remember many names and details. It's also useful for any job that requires remembering facts, and one that comes to mind is palmistry!

The Loop of Imagination and the Countryside

There are two gifts that come with this loop. The first is a good imagination, and the other is a powerful sense of intuition. If the loop is somewhat high and fairly near the mount of Mars, the person may work in the psychic sciences. When the loop is lower on the hand, the imagination is still present and the person may love music or poetry, but he will also love the countryside. If this loop is actually a whorl, the person can be too "over the top" or single-minded about the things that interest him.

❋ ❋ ❋

15

HEALTH

This subject can easily fill a book on its own, and there are several around, including some excellent translations of Chinese books. This chapter will only cover the basics. One big tip I can give you is that health issues are often more obvious on the minor hand than on the dominant one.

Hand Color

As we have already seen, a small patch of redness can indicate a shock or upheaval, but a larger area of redness is quite common. This usually appears around the percussion side of the hand and the bottom of the hand, with the affected mounts being Mercury, Mars, Luna, Neptune, and Venus. For the most part, this isn't anything to worry about, but if the area is a deep and angry red, it shows something going wrong with the lungs and heart, probably due to heavy smoking, a glandular situation, or high blood pressure.

- Hands should have a healthy color that is not too pale and not too red, and they should be in keeping with the race of their owner.
- Pale hands suggest poor circulation, especially if the fingers are somewhat grey, blue, or purple, which indicates trouble with veins and arteries.
- Yellow hands suggest jaundice.

Temperature

- Hot, sweaty hands can indicate thyroid or glandular irregularities.
- Hot, dry hands can show kidney difficulties, high blood pressure, or fever.
- Very cold hands suggest poor circulation, the onset of an illness, or a recent shock.
- Cold, clammy hands indicate liver problems.
- Cold patches denote an uneven circulation pattern or heart trouble, especially when these are on the fingers.

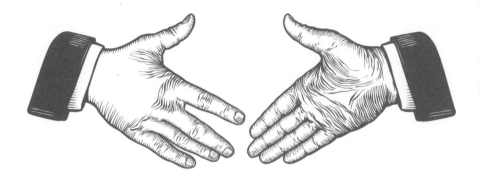

The Condition of the Hands

Older people have soft hands, but softness can also occur during pregnancy. Otherwise, this means a lack of energy and a nervous nature. It can also denote a lack of protein due to a vegan diet.

Smooth, satiny skin shows an overactive thyroid, while rough, coarse, cold, dry hands with brittle nails indicate an underactive thyroid.

Another thing worth bearing in mind is that square, robust-looking hands belong to people with good resistance to illness and good powers of recovery, while finer, thinner hands belong to a person with a weaker constitution.

The Mouse

If you ask your questioner to make a fist, you should see a slight protuberance on the back of his hand, next to the thumb and directly behind the mount of Venus. This is called the *mouse*. If the mouse is high and firm, the person is strong and robust, but if it is soft and flabby, the person is ill, weak, in pain, or perhaps just getting old.

Some Disturbances to Consider

A grille often indicates sickness or a shock to the system. It shows up on Mercury when the liver is sluggish and on the plain of Mars when the kidneys are involved or when there is some kind of digestive trouble.

A grille or any disturbance around the area of Neptune points to activity in the reproductive areas of the body. If the area is slightly red and filled with tiny lines, a woman might be pregnant or have recently given birth. There is often a kind of triangular mark on Neptune, and if one or both sides of the triangle on a woman's hand are islanded or broken, there could be something going on with her reproductive organs.

If the edge of the hand on the Venus side below the thumb is covered in small, glassy warts, the person may develop cancer. Another place to look for cancer is on the percussion beside the mount of Mercury, where small, glassy warts can show up around the attachment and child lines.

There can be a skin ridge pattern that forms a triangle on Mercury, and if it is high up on the mount, it indicates a congenital weakness of the heart or a family tendency to heart problems.

Example of a Grille

Lines and Health

The Heart Line

- Tumors in the breasts which might or might not be cancerous may be present when there is a gap in the heart line below the Apollo finger at the spot where it begins to bend upward. This could equally signal something wrong with the lungs.

- A flaky or islanded start to the heart line is fairly common, but if the line is almost obliterated by muddle, there is something amiss with the heart.
- When the flesh on either side of the line in the area of Apollo and Mercury is hard and elevated, this indicates heart problems. Dents and islands on the heart line are also bad news for the heart.
- Islands under Saturn denote something wrong with the hearing.
- A long island below Mercury denotes throat or breathing problems, while a smaller island suggests dental issues.
- Dots suggest inflammation and fever or some current health issue.

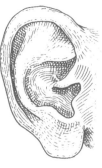

The Head Line

- Headaches and eye trouble show up as chains or tiny islands on the head line. If these are red, the problem is serious and ongoing; if they are white, it comes and goes.
- Actual physical damage to the head can be seen by disturbances on the head line. Doubled head lines, large islands, or other unusual features point to mental problems.
- An effect that looks like a pair of tongs grabbing the end of the head line, or the head line forming this kind of shape can indicate sleep problems or that the subject does not need much sleep.

The Life Line

This should be strong and unblemished if the person's health is vigorous, but life being what it is means that there are bound to be some disturbances on this line. Consider the top of the line to relate to the head and the end of it to relate to the feet; this makes it fairly easy to work out where the trouble lies.

- Fine lines that blot it out can talk of irritable bowel syndrome. Alternatively, this might be due to allergies or intolerance to wheat or lactose. Look for a via lasciva to confirm this.

The Life Line or the Fate Line

Fine lines that fall away from the bottom end of the life line or the fate line and head toward the lower end of the mount of Luna indicate diabetes. I have just this formation myself, and I have had diet-controlled type-2 diabetes for many years.

- Breaks and changes of direction in the life line are common, and they can mean a setback or change in the direction of the individual's life rather than a health problem.
- Dots, pits, and small marks on the line show pain in and around the spine in particular and the skeleton in general. A grille beside the life line can denote severe back trouble, possibly due to arthritis.
- A large, egg-shaped island near Neptune shows a disease gathering in the body, and this may turn out to be cancer.
- A gap in the life line can be caused by illness, but also by restriction and unhappiness. If the person recovers from the trauma, the gap may still sit on the minor hand as a reminder even if it vanishes from the dominant hand.

The Rascettes

The rascettes are lines that run round the wrist at the base of the hand. Old-time palmists believed that there should be three clear rascettes, each standing for thirty years of life, thus a good life span would be ninety years. I have noticed that if the upper rascette loops into the hand or breaks up, there is something wrong with the lungs or the uterus.

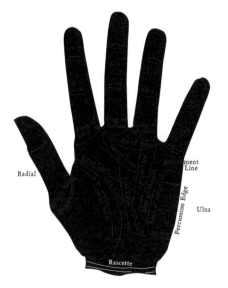

Unusual Situations

Little lines that rise up the hands and end in small forks under each finger denote chromosomal abnormalities, and if allied to a simian line and curved fingers that have wide gaps at the base, this is even more likely. Also, there may be more than the usual number of whorls on the fingertips. Check for attachment and child lines, as there may not be any of these.

Fingernails

Fingernails take about eight months to grow so they show things that have happened to the person during that period of time. This isn't a comprehensive diagnostic tool, but it does have its uses.

Fingernail Dents

Lateral dents turn up after an illness, a time of pain, or an operation. They can also register a time of emotional upset. A nail takes about eight months to grow out, so it is fairly easy to work out when the event occurred. Longitudinal dents are common in old age, as are thickened nails, which often accompany arthritis.

- If dents only appear on one or two nails, usually the thumb and the Jupiter fingernail, the problem wasn't so bad or so long-lasting.
- If dents appear on most of the nails, the individual went through a really tough time.
- The depth of the dent is also important, with the deepest usually being the result of a major wound or an operation.

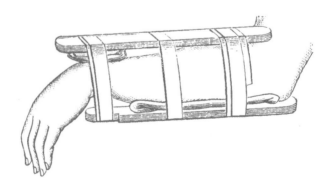

- If dents only appear on the thumb, the pain will be in the head or upper spine.
- On the Jupiter finger, the pain will be in the spine or middle part of the body.
- On the Saturn finger, the lower spine, pelvis, or hips.
- On the Apollo finger, the problem is in the legs.
- On the Mercury finger, the damage is to the lower legs, ankles, feet, arms, wrists, or hands.

Other Fingernail Disturbances

Hippocratic nails have a distinctive convex shape. They are also known as "watch glass" nails, because their domed shape is like the glass on an old-fashioned pocket watch. These were a classic indication of tuberculosis of the lungs, and in the modern day, they indicate emphysema or lung cancer. When this kind of nail is present, the fingers themselves might be club-shaped at the ends. This clears up when the problem clears up, but the Jupiter and Saturn fingers will always have slightly curled nails if the lungs are irrevocably damaged.

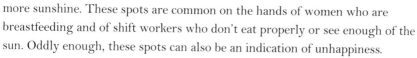

White spots on the nails are common and suggest a calcium, vitamin D, or other mineral deficiency or that the subject needs to get more sunshine. These spots are common on the hands of women who are breastfeeding and of shift workers who don't eat properly or see enough of the sun. Oddly enough, these spots can also be an indication of unhappiness.

Many ridges on the nails, especially on the thumb, may come down to nerves, but they are most likely a warning that something is affecting the heart. This could be as simple as a sensitivity to coffee, even if the subject drinks decaffeinated.

- Soft nails show a lack of calcium.
- Brittle nails mean there are nutritional deficiencies.

- Grayish and white nails indicate heart or lung disease.
- Waxy, white nails suggest that ulcers are bleeding somewhere in the body.
- Horizontal white strips near the tips show cirrhosis of the liver.
- A thin, white line across the hand can suggest Hodgkin's disease.
- Two or three arc-shaped lines across the hand show lead or arsenic poisoning. I have found that those who take a course of iron pills or a tonic medicine that contains iron will get these pale arcs on the thumbnails.
- Red/brown nails indicate kidney dysfunction.
- Upturned or spoon-shaped nails show spinal disease, alcoholism, liver damage, an underactive thyroid, or brain damage.
- Tiny nails predict weakness in the stomach, bladder, and kidneys.
- Dark patches on the nails suggest a fungal infection.
- An overgrowth of skin around the nails indicates psoriasis.
- A tunnel-shaped nail on the Mercury finger tells of spinal trouble.

The Moons

Moons are the white half-moon shapes that some
people have at the base of their nails. These should
be fairly large on the thumb and Jupiter fingers and
smaller or even missing on the other fingers.

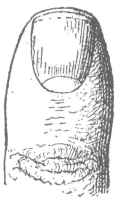

If the moons change shape or size, this could be
an indication of impending heart trouble, but if they
suddenly vanish from the fingers, the person is in
danger of a stroke or he has already had one.

According to Chinese lore, those with few moons
or very small ones need food and drink that is heated
rather than cold and they need spicy food. Those with large moons need cool
drinks, cool food, and little or no pepper, chili, or other types of hot spice.

❋ ❋ ❋

16

PREDICTION— WITH A TOUCH OF MAGIC

With this book in mind, I recently had a chat with my good friend Robin, who is a wonderful palmist. I asked him how he approached the predictive aspect of palmistry, as this is a notoriously difficult thing to do. Hand readers know that the whole of life is shown on the hands, and we also know that lines and marks can change shape, appear, or disappear over time, so predicting anything isn't easy. In this book, I have focused much more on the predictive aspects of hand reading than most books do for the simple reason that it is what most people want from the subject.

I am also well aware that it is difficult to deal with immediate problems on the hand. Robin told me that this was the moment when his psychic side tended to kick in and he would fall back on intuition, clairvoyance, and clairsentience (feelings about things) to come up with the goods. I am also aware that other good palmists use intuition and sometimes actual clairvoyance, which means being able to see things happening in their mind's eye. This gave me food for thought . . .

Hand reading is a knowledge-based skill, and as such, it shouldn't rely on intuition or psychism any more than skills like carpentry or dressmaking should. It must be said though, that hand reading, astrology, numerology, rune reading, and the tarot use a different sort of skills, and those who are drawn to the "psychic sciences" are often extremely intuitive. Many practitioners also train  as spiritual mediums, psychics, and so on while also studying their skill set. Others don't make a special effort to develop their psychic side, but it can't help developing as a direct result of the work they do. I have noticed that even those who deal with patients or clients as part of their normal working lives in even the most conventional fields often develop a certain amount of intuition, and they are all the better for it.

The Shape of Things to Come

My first suggestion comes from divination practices as tea leaf or coffee ground reading, and even such things as African bone reading or ancient Egyptian geomancy, where marks left in a patch of sand meant something to the interpreter. The idea is to read the hand normally first, then allow one's eyes to slip out of focus, as though one were gazing without really seeing. The little lines in the plain of Mars may start to move around, merge, and form patterns, which one can interpret. Some palmists can see initials in the hands when they do this, allowing them to suggest to the subject that he will soon meet someone important who has those initials in his or her name. A logo or trademark may show up, or something related to a house or perhaps a hint of a journey to a particular part of the world. It could be anything. If the reader wants a bit more inspiration, he can refer to a book on tea leaf reading or dream interpretation to find possible meanings for the shapes he sees.

Intuition and Psychism

If you are used to using tarot, oracle cards, and such things, or if you are psychic enough to practice psychometry (holding an object to see what you can pick up from it), you will be able to tap into your gifts as well as use your skill. There are many suggestions as to how this kind of psychic information transmits itself to a reader, but my belief is that the reader's spirit guides link with the subject's spiritual guides, who then pass the information down to the reader.

Many tarot readers use the cards to jump-start a reading but soon "lift up" from the cards, using clairvoyance, feelings, and even clairaudience (being able to hear spirit voices) to take the reading forward. The same can happen when reading hands, although I would advise the reader to open up psychically *after* completing the "scientific" reading, as it is hard to work on a mental vibration while also using a psychic one. My palmist friends agree that this is the best policy, although sometimes the psychic images start to kick in early, and all the reader can do is pass on the information, then take a few minutes break before going back to giving his skilled analysis.

Is it necessary to be psychic to be a palmist? No it isn't, but it can be helpful, and if you feel anything kicking in on a psychic vibration, don't push it away.

The Usual Caveat

Be careful when telling someone about their future, because even if they pretend to be skeptical, they will take in your words, and they can become unnerved or upset. If you think something bad is on the way to your questioner, it is best to say you think he may be in for some minor kind of difficulty in his love life or his health or whatever. You can suggest that he should take steps to minimize the situation, but that he shouldn't worry too much about it. In short, it would be far better for you to be wrong about the magnitude of the situation than to put frightening ideas into the mind of your subject.

Some palmists love to dramatize a reading to make it more exciting than it is, and sadly, this can even apply to some people who have been in the business for a long time. This has nothing to do with informing or helping a client, as it is entirely about the ego of the reader, and overly dramatized information can be very frightening to a client. Please be better than this. Hand reading itself is wonderful, and it doesn't need to be dressed in a kind of Halloween aura just to make the reader feel self-important.

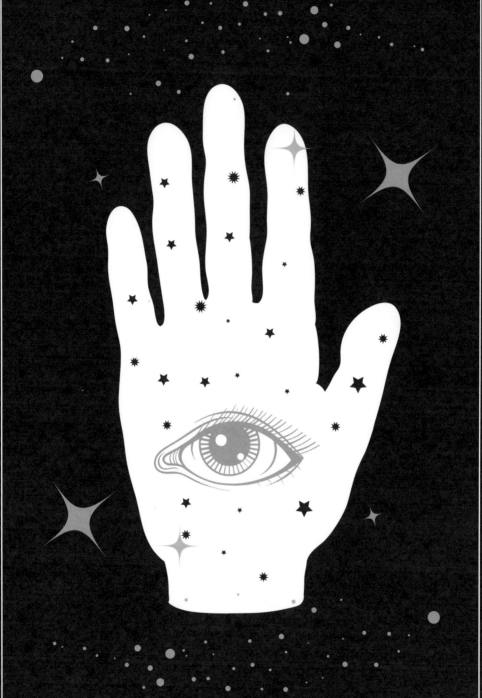

CONCLUSION

This book has given you a good basic grounding in palmistry, but you should look at many people's hands and read a variety of other books to learn the skill, because every palmist has something to bring to the subject. There is a fair bit of information on the Internet these days, and while it is often fragmented, it is useful when searching for a particular point.

As with all the psychic sciences, remember to filter everything others tell you through a layer of common sense, and to use common sense when reading or learning about it. Keep your feet on the ground while picking up information and storing it in your mind—or even taking notes. If you do, you will soon become proficient and successful in your new interest. You'll certainly be able to entertain yourself and your friends, and you might even find yourself on the way to a new career.

Hand reading was my first divination and I am still fascinated by it all these years later. While you might set it aside from time to time and do other things with your life, you'll always drift back to it, as it is so intriguing.

❊ ❊ ❊

ABOUT THE AUTHOR

Roberta Vernon's mother was vaguely into palmistry, and this sparked a childhood interest, which later became a hobby, and then a career. One of her most interesting palm reading experiences occurred when she was reading hands at a psychic festival. A client sat down and presented his hands, and when looking at them, Roberta felt certain that there was something radically wrong with the man's left leg. Not knowing whether she ought to say anything about it or not, she took the bull by the horns and urged him to consult a doctor. Her client threw his head back and laughed heartily, while pulling up his pant leg and showing Roberta a prosthetic limb! He'd lost his own leg many years before in an accident. Roberta has written dozens of articles on this subject, along with one book on palmistry and another on feng shui under her married name of Roberta Peters. She lives in England with her husband, Bob Peters. They have two children and four grandchildren.

IMAGE CREDITS

INDEX